DISCOVER THE KEYS TO STAYING FULL OF GOD

by
Andrew Wommack

Harrison House
Tulsa, Oklahoma

12 11 10 09 08   10 9 8 7 6 5 4 3

Discover the Keys to Staying Full of God
ISBN 13: 978-1-57794-934-3
ISBN 10: 1-57794-934-X
Copyright © 2008 by Andrew Wommack Ministries, Inc.
P.O. Box 3333
Colorado Springs, CO 80934-3333
www.awmi.net

Published by Harrison House Publishers
P.O. Box 35035
Tulsa, Oklahoma 74153
www.harrisonhouse.com

CONTENTS

Introduction

Growing up in church, I was taught that Christians are leaky vessels. Like a bucket full of holes, we must continually be "refilled," and according to the average believer's experience, this seems true. God touches our life and we become excited about it, but then—within a short period of time—we're back to being just as empty and needing something special from the Lord as we were before.

This was clearly illustrated to me through a woman who had been listening to my teaching. She told me she had seen the Lord's love for her greater than ever before. In fact, she was overwhelmed with God's unconditional love for her. But then she concluded, "I know this won't last long. It never does. In a month or so, I'll be back to where I was—but I'm enjoying it now!"

Although this is what most people experience, it's not what the Lord taught. He told us that we're supposed to go "from glory to glory," not pit to pit. (2 Cor. 3:18.) We aren't supposed to just struggle all the time because God's Word promises:

Every valley shall be exalted, and every mountain and hill shall be made low: and the crooked shall be made straight, and the rough places plain.

ISAIAH 40:4

Since this is the case, we ought to be enjoying some consistency in our Christian life. We don't have to have a "yo-yo" experience with God.

Ever since the Lord revealed His love to me on March 23, 1968, I've been one excited and turned-on guy for Him. I've had much opposition and many bad things happen to me, but it's never stolen what God said. Satan has definitely done his best to derail me, but I've never lost the joy of what the Lord did in my heart. In fact, it's actually stronger today than it was back in 1968 when it first happened. My revelation and experience of God's love is even better now than when I first had that awe-inspiring, life-changing encounter with Him.

Although this isn't the experience of most believers—it can be yours. You can enjoy consistency and stability in your Christian life, too.

Who's the Variable?

Romans 11:29 reveals that:

The gifts and calling of God *are* without repentance.

Therefore, the Lord isn't the One who comes and goes in your life. You do perceive His presence, anointing, joy, and other benefits that come from Him stronger at times, but it's not God giving and then withdrawing from you. Very few people understand this.

Most Christians bombard heaven, crying, "Oh God, what's wrong? Please touch my life again. I want a fresh touch from You. Lord, please come and do something new in my life today!"

When you pray that way, you're insulting God. You're assuming that whenever you feel dry and empty, whenever you lose your peace, joy, or whatever, that God is the One who withdrew from you. Not true!

Once you're born again, God never changes toward you—ever. He's always releasing—transmitting—His presence, blessing, anointing, joy, healing, prosperity and all that He is into your life. The Lord never changes, but you do. You must understand this as we begin looking into how to stay full of God.

Popular teaching today insinuates that the reason you aren't walking in God's love, peace, joy, etc., is because you've done something to displease Him. Therefore, it mainly centers on what you can do to "please" God and get His power flowing in your life again. This is never the case because the Lord has never withdrawn from you.

God isn't the variable—you are. So, everything I'm going to share centers on how you can fix you. This won't be a lesson on how to bombard the gates of heaven and "make" God do something. He's already done everything through the death, burial, and resurrection of the Lord Jesus Christ. God wants you blessed even more than you do!

As Full As You Want to Be

Right now, you are as full of God as you believe to be. He doesn't determine how full of love, joy, and peace you are. You do. God is always willing for every single person to be healed, delivered, and prospered. It's never the Lord who doesn't move in your life—it's you who aren't receiving from Him. That's why I want to encourage you in how to receive.

Wherever you are right now, there are television signals around you. You may not be able to perceive them, but they are there. If you plugged in, turned on, and tuned in a television set, you could perceive the signal. When you turned on your receiver to experience the sight and sound of the picture, that isn't when the broadcast began. It's just when you started receiving.

That's the way it is with the Lord. God is healing every person who ever needs to be healed. He's giving love, joy, and peace to you constantly. The transmitters of heaven are beaming twenty-four hours a day, every day of the week. God is never the One who's not blessing you. You're the one who has either turned off or not tuned in.

I'm for revival, but the way most people are seeking it isn't the way it's going to happen. Praying, "Oh God, send revival!" and believing that it's up to Him how much of it we experience is wrong. It's not God's fault that there isn't more of an outpouring of His power and Spirit in our land. He hasn't stopped pouring out the Holy Spirit upon believers since the day of Pentecost. We just aren't very good receivers. We're the ones who are short-circuiting God's power and blessing in our lives. The Lord wants massive worldwide revival. He wants everyone to receive salvation. But since we aren't turned on and tuned in to Him, we aren't receiving like we should.

Fix Your Receiver

"Oh God, fix Your transmitter! Oh Lord, why aren't You sending revival? What's wrong with You? Don't You care? If we get thousands of people to fast and pray with us, maybe we can twist Your arm and motivate You to do something." What an ungodly attitude.

"The Lord is ticked off at America. He's up in heaven with His arms folded, frowning and saying, 'I'm not going to do anything else for you until you repent and grovel in the dirt some more.'" Wrong! People who say things like that don't really believe that God is good.

These things I'm sharing would get me kicked out of many churches. Begging for revival and pleading for God to move are common attitudes and practices in American Christianity today. However, you need to know that God isn't the One holding anything back. He's transmitting everything Jesus Christ provided through His death, burial, and resurrection.

If you aren't full of God today, it's you who have chosen it. Even though you may strongly desire to stay full of God, you've made choices that have prevented you from receiving and manifesting His love, joy, peace, healing, prosperity, and other blessings. However, there's good news.

God's Word shows us four things we can do to fix our receiver. That's why I wrote this book.

CHAPTER 1

Intuitive Revelation

For I am not ashamed of the gospel of Christ: for it is the power of God unto salvation to every one that believeth; to the Jew first, and also to the Greek. For therein is the righteousness of God revealed from faith to faith: as it is written, The just shall live by faith.

ROMANS 1:16,17

This word *gospel* is a radical term. Prior to and outside of the Bible, we only have two examples of this Greek word *euaggelion*, which was translated "gospel,"[1]being used in Greek literature. That's because it's a superlative. It actually means more than just good news. It means too-good-to-be-true news or "glad tidings."[2]Since there was virtually nothing too good to be true until Jesus came, it was hardly ever used.

But once Jesus came along, they started using *gospel* to refer to what He was preaching and demonstrating: God isn't judging people. He's not even angry anymore. For instance, the Lord extended mercy to the harlot taken in the act of adultery. (John 8:3–11.) Christ's message and the way He loved people unconditionally were both too good to be true!

The Jews of Jesus' time were very religious. They had been raised under a works-oriented, performance-based, legalistic, judgmental religious system. Therefore, they persecuted anyone who preached the true gospel. Why? The gospel—salvation by grace through faith in the Lord Jesus Christ—was just too good to be true.

So when Paul said it's the gospel—this too-good-to-be-true news of the Lord's unconditional love—that is the power of God to change people's lives, the religious folks' immediate response was, "Well then, what about God's wrath? You need to let people know there's a hell, that God is just, and He's going to send people there. You need to use fear to scare people out of hell." That was the religious concept of the day.

The Goodness of God

Hell is a real place, and I do tell people about it. Those who don't believe on the Lord Jesus Christ will go there because that's the choice they made, but that's not the core message of Christianity. It's a truth, but it's not good news, and it's definitely not the gospel.

God's goodness—not the fear of hell—is what leads people to repentance. (Rom. 2:4.) However, the message of the American church has been for so long, "Believe on Jesus so you won't go to hell." That's the wrong message. It's a true message, but it's not the gospel. The good news that truly releases God's power and draws people to Him in droves is the gospel: God is good and He loves you. Through Christ's atonement, everything you need for abundant life—both in heaven to come and on earth here and now—has already been provided. All you must do is believe and receive. This is what we should be preaching.

For an in-depth study of the gospel, as revealed through the book of Romans, please refer to my teaching entitled "The Gospel: The Power of God."

The Homing Device

"But Andrew, what about the wrath of God?" Paul addressed this in Romans 1:18–20.

For the wrath of God is revealed.

ROMANS 1:18

You could say, "For the wrath of God is already revealed." In other words, the reason why you don't have to preach the wrath of God is because people already know in their heart that they aren't in right standing with Him. That's why they're afraid of death. In their heart, they know their eternity is on the line and they aren't sure how they relate to God.

> For the wrath of God is revealed from heaven against all ungodliness and unrighteousness of men, who hold the truth in unrighteousness, because that which may be known of God is manifest in them; for God hath [past tense] shewed *it* unto them.
>
> ROMANS 1:18,19

This is saying that the Creator placed within His creation a homing device. There is an intuitive revelation of the existence of God on the inside of every human being who has ever breathed on this earth. Some may argue, "Oh no, that's not so. I don't believe there is a God. I don't feel Him. I have no conviction, no awareness of God at all. He's never touched me. I'm totally godless." They're lying through their teeth! How do I know? I believe God's Word more than what people say.

As an American soldier serving in Vietnam, some of my comrades told me, "I'm an atheist. I don't believe in God." However, once those bombs began dropping and the bullets started to fly, those "atheists" cried out to this God they didn't believe in for mercy at the top of their lungs.

The truth is every person who has ever breathed has a revelation of the existence of God.

Without Excuse

Verse 20 goes on to say:

> For the invisible things of him from the creation of the world are clearly seen [not obscurely or vaguely, but clearly seen], being understood by the things that are made, *even* his eternal power and Godhead; so that they are without excuse.

No one will ever stand before God and say, "But I never heard. I never knew You existed!" Even if they haven't heard a preacher preach to them, they've had this inner witness and they'll be accountable according to the revelation they have. This is true of every person.

When atheists tell me, "I don't believe in God," I just go ahead and talk to them as if they do. They say, "I told you, I don't believe in God" and I answer, "I know what you said, but it's not true. You're lying." I've kept talking like this to many people who have claimed not to believe in God. Somewhere in the conversation, I end up pricking this little part of them that already had this knowledge of God. Then—all of a sudden—they open up and start admitting it.

Psalm 46:10 says:

> Be still, and know that I *am* God.

When you get still, you can hear this homing device. When you aren't occupied with anything, it'll start drawing you to God. That's the reason why—prior to salvation—people don't like to be still. They call it being "bored" or "lonely" among other things. Although they use many different terms to describe it, this homing device in their heart is what's speaking to them.

What does it say? "You know this isn't right. You shouldn't be living this way. There has to be more to life than this. Where did I come from? Where am I going? Who created me?" In order to drown this out and ignore it, they have to saturate their eyes and ears with radio and television. They must constantly keep themselves busy with something or this homing device will talk to them and convict them over their lifestyle.

Progressive Steps

Everyone already has a revelation of God. You were born with it, and it stays with you throughout your entire life.

But the rest of Romans 1, beginning with verse 21, reveals progressive steps you can take that will diminish or stop this intuitive knowledge of God from drawing you home to Him. You can actually reach a place where your heart becomes hardened so much over a period of time that you can't hear this homing device—this revelation of God—anymore. Romans 1:21 and following talk about these progressive steps you must take in order to walk away from this revelation.

Since you are reading this book, you've probably already received the Lord. So it's not like you are walking away from the intuitive knowledge of God in your heart. However, these principles apply to everything God does in your life. They don't just work before you were saved concerning God's existence. Before you lose the benefit of anything the Lord has done in your life, you must pass through these four steps.

These four keys in Romans 1:21 describe the steps you take both to walk away from and to draw near to God. Take, for instance, the joy of the Lord. Perhaps it's not as strong today as it once was in your life. If you've ever known God's love, but you aren't experiencing it today as you did once before, there were steps you took away from Him. These are also the same steps you use to come back to Him.

Let's say the revelation is healing. Perhaps you've been healed, but now it seems like you've lost that healing and you're back to where you were before. God didn't quit transmitting His healing power—you just stopped receiving. You've done at least one of these four things listed in Romans 1:21.

The Four Keys

We could continue right on through the rest of Romans 1, starting in verse 22, and bring out many other important truths. But we're going to limit the scope of this study to the four keys to staying full of God revealed in verse 21.

> Because that, when they knew God, [1]they glorified *him* not as God, [2] neither were thankful; but [3] became vain in their imaginations, and [4] their foolish heart was darkened.
>
> ROMANS 1:21

Expressed negatively, as in this verse, the four keys are:

1.   They glorified *him* not as God

2.   Neither were thankful

3.   Became vain in their imaginations

4.   Their foolish heart was darkened

These same four keys expressed positively are:

1.   Glorify God

2.   Be thankful

3.   Recognize the power of your imagination

4.   Have a good heart

Depending on how you walk out these four progressive steps in your everyday life, *you* decide whether—or not—you stay full of God.

CHAPTER 2

The Place of Importance

When God touches your life, Satan immediately comes to steal it away. (Mark 4:15.) He doesn't want you to keep whatever it was the Lord gave you—a revelation, a blessing, a healing, for instance. The Enemy does this by trying to get you to quit glorifying God as God. If you stop glorifying God as God—and stop glorifying what He's done in your life—then you'll lose the manifestation of that revelation, blessing, healing, or whatever else was manifested. It'll seem like your joy and peace are diminishing. But if you don't quit glorifying God and what He's done in your life, you'll never lose it—and it'll increase.

So then, what does it mean to "glorify" God?

When I first ran across this, I looked it up in the *Strong's* concordance. The Greek word used in Romans 1:21 for *glorify* means "to render (or esteem) glorious."[1]That didn't help me very much.

So I looked up both *render* and *esteem* in the dictionary. It was when I saw the definition for *esteem* that God opened my eyes to this truth. *Esteem* means "to value, to prize, or to reverence."[2]

You Place Value on Everything

When God does something in your life, you place a value upon it, but then Satan immediately comes against that value and competes for it. He tries to steal from you the worth and value you've placed on the things of God. This happens to everyone.

The same thing will happen with this teaching. Some people who read this will receive it. Others won't. But one way or another, you are placing a value on what you're learning.

When ye received the word of God which ye heard of us, ye received *it* not *as* the word of men, but as it is in truth, the word of God, which effectually worketh also in you that believe.

1 THESSALONIANS 2:13

Some readers will say, "This is God speaking to me" and others will conclude "That's just Andrew." Then you'll place a value on these truths and they'll affect your life—or not—accordingly.

You place a value on everything that comes into your life. The devil comes immediately to attack the value you place on God, His Word, and the manifestation of what He's done—and doing—in your life.

It's Your Choice

Let's say the Lord speaks to you and reveals His unconditional love. You experience and feel that love saying, "God loves me! Almighty God loves me!" You receive the peace, joy, and other benefits that revelation and experience bring, but tomorrow the devil will agitate someone at work to come over and dump on you. They'll tell you what an absolute zero you are, criticizing your performance or something else the devil knows will bother you. Do you know what's happening? The Enemy is competing for the value you placed on God and His love.

You can go to church and get so blessed and happy. Then you go home and someone jumps all over your case. Satan is trying to steal your joy. Here's what God says about you and here's the opposite. It's like a seesaw according to the value you place on it. When one side is up, the other side is down—and vice versa. If you value what God says, then you have to devalue what others say. Like a seesaw, you can't have both sides up at the same time. "God loves me. Not only does He love me, He likes me. He's pleased with me. I'm full of joy unspeakable and full of glory!"

But when the criticism and opposition come, will you hold on to what God has said and done, or will you start honoring, prizing, and valuing the acceptance of those people equal to or above God? If you let their word have power and increase, then the value you place on God's Word and what He's done in your life will decrease. You'll start losing the manifestation of joy, peace, and victory that revelation gave you. It wasn't God who quit transmitting it, but you who quit receiving. You allowed something else to occupy the position in your life that was meant for God.

You place a value on everything that comes against you. No one else can. Nobody else can dictate the worth you place on something in your life. It's your choice.

Love and Hate

Your spouse, child, or boss says something to you that upsets you. Let's say it just really ticked you off. However, if they said the exact same words to me, it would have a different effect. Why? I don't value their opinion the way you do.

"But I'm supposed to value my spouse, child, or boss's opinion." Yes, you should value them more than I do—but in a relative sense. The Lord said:

> If any *man* come to me, and hate not his father, and mother, and wife, and children, and brethren, and sisters, yea, and his own life also, he cannot be my disciple.
>
> LUKE 14:26

> He that loveth father or mother more than me is not worthy of me: and he that loveth son or daughter more than me is not worthy of me.
>
> MATTHEW 10:37

Your love for even your immediate family ought to pale in comparison to your love for Jesus. The contrast between the worth and value you place on God and others should be as different as love and hate. Of course, you should value certain people who are closer to you more than I do. But in comparison to God and what He's done in your life, you ought to place such a value and worth upon Him that nothing and no one ever competes. However, this isn't the way most Christians operate.

Do you glorify the things of God more than the things of this world? Is the difference so small that I'd have to use a magnifying glass to see which you truly value the most? It ought to be obvious. Compared to how you esteem God, you should disesteem—decrease the worth and value on—everything and everyone else.

Greater Than Your Mate

We've actually become codependent on everyone and everything else except God. If your mate were to leave you, would you fall apart like a two-dollar suitcase? I agree that it's God's best for your marriage to be healed and made whole. Of course, the Lord wants to move in that area of your life. But what if your spouse doesn't cooperate? You need to make a commitment and say, "God, You are so much greater than my mate. If things don't work out and they leave, I won't miss a stride. I'll keep praising, loving, and serving You with all my heart—even if everyone forsakes me. You're awesome!"

Moses' wife left him for a year or two. Zipporah took off when they were on their way down to Egypt, but Moses just kept moving forward with the Lord. (Ex. 18:2.) The plagues were released, the children of Israel were delivered, and the Red Sea parted. All this happened while he was separated from his wife.

Some people think, "Well, brother, I believe I'm supposed to love and value God, but you can't praise Him while going through a divorce." Sure you can.

A partner of mine in Charlotte, North Carolina, used to have me in to his business each year. He'd tell his employees, "The clock is running. You listen to this guy for as long as he wants to talk." Then I'd just share with them the goodness of God. I did this for many years.

While in the break room after I had spoken once, a certain lady came over to talk to me. She was an alcoholic who had tried to kill herself. She'd slit her wrists and wound up in the hospital. She was going through her third or fourth divorce and was very poor. Everything in her life was depressing and discouraging.

"Who Cares?"

She told me, "Andrew, I'm not a Christian like you and Chip (my friend, the business owner), but I know that prayer works. I want prayer for my marriage." Then she broke down and started to cry. She told me it was her third or fourth marriage, and that her husband had filed for a divorce. If she got divorced again, she didn't know if she could make it. So she wanted me to pray for her marriage.

I stopped her and asked, "Now let me make sure I heard you right. You aren't a Christian and you know it."

"That's right."

"If you were to die right now, you would go straight to hell."

"That's correct."

"And you want me to pray for your marriage and not your salvation?"

"Yes."

I said, "Lady, do you realize that after you've burned in hell for a thousand years, you won't give a rip whether you were ever married or not? Who cares about your marriage—you need to be born again!"

She responded, "You know what? You're right!" So I prayed with her and she was born again.

I'm not saying that God isn't concerned about your marriage, but you must look at it in terms of its relative worth. Compared to eternity, marriage is nothing. It's all about the value you place on things.

Jesus Disesteemed

Some people place so much value on their marriage, career, and other people's acceptance that it honestly competes for the worth they've placed on the things of God. If that's you, you need to make a decision and say, "Lord, there is nothing that could even remotely tempt me to ever decrease the value I place on You and what You've done in my life." Then you need to magnify and glorify God, and disesteem everything else.

Wherefore seeing we also are compassed about with so great a cloud of witnesses, let us lay aside every weight, and the sin which doth so easily beset *us*, and let us run with patience the race that is set before us, looking unto Jesus the author and finisher of *our* faith; who for the joy that was set before him endured the cross, *despising the shame*, and is set down at the right hand of the throne of God.

HEBREWS 12:1,2

Notice the phrase "despising the shame." The Greek word rendered *despising* literally means "to disesteem."[3] It's the exact opposite of esteeming, glorifying, magnifying, valuing, and prizing. Jesus *disesteemed* the shame associated with what He had to go through.

You cannot truly glorify God and everything else at the same time. It's like that seesaw we talked about. Both ends can't be up at the same time. You must esteem one and disesteem everything else. Jesus disesteemed the shame associated with His crucifixion. He intentionally minimized and shrunk the cost.

That's not the way most of us function. If you or I had been called on by God to suffer crucifixion, we probably would have immediately looked at the shame, cost, and pain. We would have valued our own life, peace, and security in such a way that we wouldn't have been able to value what God called us to do.

But Jesus had already disesteemed His own life. (Phil. 2:5–8.) He viewed everything else as worthless compared to what God had said and done.

Dung!

Paul did the same:

> But what things were gain to me, those I *counted* loss for Christ. Yea doubtless, and I *count* all things *but* loss for the excellency of the knowledge of Christ Jesus my Lord: for whom I have suffered the loss of all things, and do *count* them *but* dung, that I may win Christ.
>
> PHILIPPIANS 3:7,8

You place a value on everything in your life. You are the one who esteems what's important to you. Paul said, "I placed a high value on knowing Christ and disesteemed everything else as if it were dung." That's a strong statement.

Most Christians can't say that—which is the reason we can't do what Paul did. It's also why we don't have the same joy. Paul wrote the book of Philippians while in prison. Yet, it's his happiest book. He used the words "joy," "rejoice," and "rejoicing" a total of seventeen times in just four chapters. Paul was praising God and rejoicing from jail.

If you were thrown in prison this evening, would you be singing and praising the Lord at midnight? Probably not.

You place so much value and worth on your life, freedom, and possessions. You've put so much value on things that are unimportant. Your life is important, but compared to God it's worth nothing. You need to place a relative worth on your life. As long as you are the center of your universe, you are always going to be upset when someone rubs you the wrong way. If you are all wrapped up in yourself, you make a very small package.

Meant for God

Paul had a different value system. He actually struggled with whether to stay here or go to heaven.

> For to me to live *is* Christ, and to die *is* gain...For I am in a strait betwixt two, having a desire to depart, and to be with Christ; which is far better: Nevertheless to abide in the flesh *is* more needful for you.
>
> PHILIPPIANS 1:21,23,24

Paul didn't count his life here as anything. He's the one who placed this value on it.

You're the one who places value on everything that comes into your life. I remember climbing a trail on Pikes Peak with a friend of mine. He started telling me about a mutual friend who had said some very negative things about both of us. I told him I didn't want to hear it. We had discussed this before, and I didn't care to hear the latest thing this guy had criticized me over. My friend became quiet for a while and then asked, "Why doesn't what he says about you bother you the way his criticism of me bothers me?" I answered, "It's because I don't value his opinion of me the way you value his opinion of you." It's all about the value you place on things.

The reason you begin to lose the revelation, blessing, and benefit of what God has said and done is that you've placed value on so many other things instead of Him. These other things that are important to you are sapping your time, energy, and attention. Due to this, what the Lord has done in your life has diminished over time. It's not because God changed His attitude toward you and quit giving. It's because you've let something else occupy that place of importance in your life that was meant for God alone.

CHAPTER 3

"God Loves Me!"

God supernaturally revealed His love to me in a Saturday night prayer meeting. It was March 23, 1968, and I was eighteen years old. All of a sudden, I knew that God passionately loved me. I understood that He carried my picture in His wallet and had an 8x10 of me on His mantle. God's unconditional love was no longer an abstract concept to me—it was real! For the next four and a half months, I literally experienced God's supernatural love transforming my life.

I was so excited that the very next morning I stood up in front of my denominational church and told them, "God loves me! He doesn't just love me from a distance, but God passionately loves me. He's pleased with me and even likes me!" It would have been better if I had cussed. They would've been more merciful on me if I had gone out and committed adultery. At least that could be forgiven. But they equated my testimony of God loving me passionately as me claiming to have some great virtue. Since they didn't understand grace, they thought God's love was based on performance. They interpreted what I was sharing as me thinking I was better than them. So the criticism came immediately.

Someone walked up to me and asked, "Who do you think you are? You said you're filled with the Spirit."

"God did fill me with His Spirit. That's what it felt like to me. In Ephesians 5:18, Paul told us to be filled with the Spirit."

"Yeah, but that was Paul. Who do you think you are? Are you putting yourself in the same category as Paul?"

"I'm just telling you what happened."

Satan was using this seminary professor and all these educated people who did this for a living to criticize me. He was trying to get me—an eighteen-year-old boy—to value man's opinion more than what God had revealed to me.

"I Don't Care What You Say"

I was so overwhelmed with God's love that I hardly slept at night. I'd sleep a few minutes, and then I'd be awake thinking about how God loves me. Then I'd read the Word until I passed out again. I didn't sleep for more than an hour at a time for four and a half months. I don't remember ever sitting down to a meal that entire time either. Who could eat or sleep knowing that God loves them? I was excited!

There I was, valuing the fact that God loved me. When another voice came, would I value it the same? If I had begun placing value on that, then my value, worth, and reverence for what God had said would have started coming down and I would have begun losing the revelation of it. This wasn't because of some great strength of my own. I didn't even know how hungry for God I was before He touched my life. But once I experienced His awesome love and acceptance, I knew that nothing would ever excite me more. I immediately put God above everything and disesteemed anything else.

When these people—whom I respected and had tried to please and gain their acceptance—started ragging on me, I just turned away. I said, "Look, I don't care what you say!" I maintained the same relative worth and value on the things of God. Because of this, God's supernatural, unconditional love that He had given me didn't diminish.

I was a freshman math major in college at the time, but once I fell head over heels in love with God, I lost all interest in both math and college. In fact, I got to where I hated it. I went to school every day for two and a half months, but never made it to a single class. Somewhere along the way, I'd start talking to somebody about the Lord. That's what I loved to do—tell others how God loved me and how He loved them also. I wanted them to know that God could change their life too. Although the bell would ring, I couldn't let this person I was talking to go to hell just because of that. So I'd just keep right on sharing with them and miss class Then I'd talk to somebody else and another bell would ring. This went on for two and a half months!

After awhile, I thought, *Why am I paying money to go to school if I don't like it and never make it to class?* So I prayed about it and the Lord told me to quit. Now, that's not for everybody. You might need an education to do what God is calling you to do. But I didn't need to be a math major to do what I'm doing today. .

Relative Worth

Things got really bad once I announced my decision to everyone. Quitting school meant I was giving up $350 a month in social security payments from my father's death. Since this was during the height of the Vietnam War, I had a deferment for as long as I stayed in school, but if I quit, I instantly had an all expense paid trip to Vietnam. Everyone kept telling me, "This isn't smart. It's not what you're supposed to do!"

My mother didn't understand it. She wasn't mean or against me, but she couldn't believe that this was God. (My dad died when I was twelve, so Mom and I had a special bond—and we still do to this day.) Satan tried to get me to value my relationship with my mother more than I valued God, but for me, nothing in my life competes with God. My mother didn't die for me. She didn't go to hell and rise from the dead for the forgiveness of my sin. I love my mother, but I love God infinitely more.

"But Andrew, I could never make a distinction. I love God and my mother (spouse, children, friends) the same." No, you can't do that. Your love for God ought to make your love for your parents, spouse, children, and friends look like hate in comparison. (Luke 14:26.) I'm not saying to actually hate them. You should love them, but your love and intimacy with the Lord should far surpass it.

We run into problems when our relative worth for these things and God are too close. We value relationships, the recognition of others, and our career. These things are okay in their proper place, but what if loving, following, and speaking for God costs you relationships, career, or acceptance? Would you do whatever the Lord asked you, or would your relative worth of these things and God be too close?

There is nothing of relative worth to me that even comes close to God. My wife knows I love the Lord far more than I love her. I also know that she loves Him much more than she loves me. Instead of this detracting from our relationship, it's a plus. If Jamie only loved me according to how I treated her, she would have left me a long time ago.

Misunderstood

I've put my wife through the wringer backwards. It's been tough being a minister's wife and going through some of the things we've been through.

I was visiting with a minister once who had committed adultery, spent time in a mental hospital, was an alcoholic, and used drugs before he was born again. Although he'd been through some really terrible things, the Lord changed his life and turned him around. After telling me about his background, he asked me to give my testimony. So I told him about some of the poverty, hardship, and pain we'd gone through. I shared how my wife went two weeks without a stitch of food—a forced fast—while eight months pregnant. This guy stood up and declared, "My God, you were more ungodly than I ever thought about being. That's the worst testimony I've ever heard!" In many ways, that's true.

If Jamie just loved me for who I was, she would not have stayed married to me for very long. It's her commitment to God that keeps her loving me, and it's my commitment to the Lord that keeps me loving her. Loving God doesn't distract from our relationship—it improves it.

Most people are codependent upon their little world they've created. If something were to happen and it looked like they'd lose their marriage, kids, wealth, home, respect, fame, or whatever, they'd come crashing down emotionally. Why? They place such value and importance on these things.

When I first received the revelation of God's love, my mother didn't understand. The Enemy was tempting me to look at what this experience was costing me. I lost the recognition of my church. The people I looked up to were criticizing and rejecting me. My own mother went two weeks without talking to me. It wasn't that she hated me. She just flat didn't know what to say.

Finally, I took her out to eat and forced her to say something. Mom broke down crying and said, "I'm just so ashamed by what you're doing!" What she said wasn't positive, but negative. Satan was trying to get me to value that relationship above what the Lord had said. But by His grace, I always believed my relationship with my mother would work out, and it did. Things turned around after the Lord appeared to her in a dream. She worked for me twenty-one years until she finally retired for the last time at age eighty-eight. Mom is a real blessing. But whether it would have worked out or not, I wasn't going to let it affect the value I placed on what God did in my life.

At one time or another, the Lord has touched you in a significant way. Then Satan came at you in a myriad of ways in order to get you to place value on something other than God. He attacked that Word and the worth you placed on it in an attempt to get your identity off of what God said. If you've lost the manifestation of your joy, peace, healing, or revelation, it's because—somewhere along the way—you quit glorifying God.

Drafted

After dropping out of college, I was immediately required to take a preinduction physical for the Army. I passed. Then a recruiter came to my house, opened his briefcase, pulled out a bunch of papers, and started telling me all the benefits of volunteering over being drafted.

I looked at him and said, "I could save us both a lot of time."

"How's that?"

"Well, the reason I was sent to this preinduction physical and classified 1A is because I quit school."

"That's right."

"God told me to quit school." He smirked. "Therefore, it's His responsibility. If the Lord wants me drafted, I'll be drafted, and if He doesn't, I won't."

Breaking out in laughter, this recruiter told me, "Boy, I can guarantee you that you're going to Vietnam."

That made me mad. Since this guy didn't value God the way I did, he was saying the equivalent of, "Who is God compared to the United States government? Our government is stronger than God. He can't keep you from being drafted." If I had accepted that value, then immediately I would have begun to lose some of the joy and peace from what God had done in my life.

This fellow was thirty-something years old and representing the United States government. I was just a nineteen-year-old boy. But I stood up, put my finger in his chest, and said, "Listen, buddy. If God wants me drafted, I'll be drafted. If He doesn't, then neither you nor the United States government nor every demon in hell can draft me." He just stood up, gathered his things, and walked out the door. In the morning, I had my draft notice. I bet that guy processed and hand delivered it to my mailbox himself. I didn't care. I believed what I told him was true.

"But Andrew, I'm not sure I'd do something if it meant I'd be drafted and required to go to war." Well, I placed such a value on the truth that God loved me that I was willing to die for it. The cost didn't matter to me. I didn't care. I'd rather die and go be with the Lord than live my life separated from Him. I didn't give a rip about going to Vietnam. That's why I can truthfully say that since 1968, I've never lost the joy of what God did in my life. My very worst day since then has been better than my best prior to it. God is good!

Home Base

I've had terrible things happen in my life, but they've just been momentary flashes. Any discouragement or depression I've felt has never lasted more than an hour or so. Since 1968, there hasn't been a full day that I haven't had peace and joy. Why? I place value and worth on the fact that God loves me.

As a kid in Arlington, Texas, we often played a game called "Wolf and Sheep." The "wolf " had to capture the "sheep" and put them in jail. While the wolf was away, other sheep could come and set the prisoners free. The sheep had a home base. Often, home base was a tree. Whenever the sheep were touching home base, they were safe. The wolf couldn't do anything to them and had to leave.

God is my Home Base. Whenever something bad happens, I just retreat and say, "Lord, You love me. Father,

You value me. You're pleased with me." I start thinking about how much God loves me and it makes every problem I have just melt away in comparison. Satan can't touch me when I'm valuing God's love for me.

I've spent a huge amount of time glorifying—esteeming, placing value and worth on—what God has done in my life. Because of that, it's only grown stronger and better.

The reason you're a leaky vessel is because you aren't valuing what God has done in your life above all else. You're esteeming other things equal to, close to, or greater than the Lord and His opinion of you. You need to get to a place where you can honestly say, "God, You're more important to me than anyone or anything else. Nothing will compete with You." Intentionally glorify God and disesteem everything else.

Focus on the Joy

Jesus disesteemed the shame that accompanied His crucifixion.

> For the joy that was set before him [he] endured the cross, despising the shame.
>
> HEBREW 12:2

31

Jesus chose to focus on the joy. Most of us would have had such short-term thinking in that situation that we wouldn't have seen any joy in it. But Jesus looked ahead to the resurrection. He knew the cross wasn't going to be the end. He knew that He would triumph over Satan and liberate the human race. The Lord looked down through eternity and saw you and me. He saw our bondages, hurts, pains, sicknesses, diseases, and poverty. He said in His heart, "I'm going to die to redeem them. I'm going to bring them joy." He chose to magnify and glorify that, and to disesteem the shame, rejection, and physical suffering. He chose to disesteem the fact that they were going to strip Him naked, mock Him, and insult Him. He chose to minimize those things and maximize the other. He's the One who placed that value on it.

You are the one who determines the value of everything in your life. You choose how you esteem or disesteem anything and everything. Once that lady in North Carolina put a relative value on her divorce, she decided receiving the Lord was much more important. Then she began to magnify and glorify that. You're the one who determines that you can't live with or without all these things—but you can always change your determination.

CHAPTER 4

What Do You Value?

For I speak to you Gentiles, inasmuch as I am the apostle
of the Gentiles, I magnify mine office.

ROMANS 11:13

This Greek word rendered *magnify* here is the same
one translated "glorify" in Romans 1:21.[1] So, "magnify" and
"glorify" can be used interchangeably. They're the same
thing. To glorify God is to magnify Him. To magnify is to
make bigger.

Did you know that you can make God bigger? Technically
speaking, you can't affect His actual size and greatness. God
is who He is, regardless of what you think. However, as far
as your perception and experience of Him goes, you can
make God bigger or smaller in your life. It all depends on
how you think.

When you look through the small end and out the big
end of a set of binoculars, everything becomes bigger. But

if you turned it around and looked through the big end and out the little end, everything would become smaller. Although it's the same binoculars, your view enlarges or shrinks according to how you use it.

Your mind is like a pair of binoculars. Depending on the choices you make and the things you focus on, you can either magnify God and diminish your problems—or vice versa. The sad truth is that most of us have become masters at making the smallest, most insignificant things bigger and minimizing God and His Word. In our negativity, we focus on and magnify the tiny little toothpick the devil puts in our path. By the time you're finished thinking about what could happen and so forth, it's become a huge baseball bat that Satan uses to beat your brains out. But you're the one who magnified it and made it so big.

What's Bothering You?

Recently one of our Bible college students wanted to see me. He came into my office and began to cry. Since something always seemed to bother him, I asked, "What's wrong now?" It was a Monday, and he had attended church the day before. He said, "I was so hungry to hear God's Word, but the two women who were sitting in front of me talked and laughed throughout the entire service. They distracted me!"

Then he broke down weeping about how the devil had used this to steal away the Word.

I had just gotten off the phone with a friend of mine. He'd just lost his wife of nearly fifty years. I'd called to minister to him, but he was glorifying and magnifying the Lord, saying, "God is so great. God is so good. I love Him so much!" His mate of almost half a century had just died, but he was praising and thanking God right in the midst of a difficult situation.

Yet, here was this other guy sitting in my office crying because he missed hearing a message. Two women talked and he was ready to give up. That's stupid. Why didn't he just get up and move, or ask them to be quiet? This wasn't a big deal until he magnified it.

What's bothering you today? A year from now, you probably won't even remember it. Even if the Lord doesn't intervene and fix this situation you're so upset about, in twelve months you'll forget it. Why? It's insignificant. It's not really a problem. You're just magnifying it.

When people come up to me in prayer lines and tell me their problem, sometimes I literally have to bite my lip to keep from laughing. I want to say, "This is it? This is the big problem that's derailed you? I've had worse things happen on my good days!"

Honestly, some of the things people get so upset over are nothing. I'd like to buy them a one-way ticket to some third-world country I've been to where they can see first-hand what true hardship and suffering is really like. They'd return with a whole new perspective—and they'd magnify things very differently.

Misplaced Values

We talk about how kids have it so hard today. They whine if they don't have the newest model television. Life isn't difficult on our children. This is the easiest generation that has ever been.

Thomas A. Crapper was born in England in 1836. When he was eleven years old, his parents gave him a sack with some clothes and one day's food supply in it. They told him they loved him, patted him on the back, and sent him on his way. He walked 165 miles to London. He had no relatives or anyone else to look out for him. He was on his own—live or die, sink or swim. He didn't have a government sponsored social system the way we do today. He couldn't exist on welfare. He could have died. Thomas was on his own at eleven years of age!

I couldn't imagine one of my kids being out on their own and trying to make their way in life at eleven years old. *This had to be unusual.* The next paragraph said this was very unusual. Most kids didn't leave home until they were twelve. If you were a twelve-year-old in England in the 1840s, you were on your own to make your way in life as an adult—live or die, sink or swim. Now that's pressure!

Not having designer jeans, the newest video game, or being able to watch MTV isn't pressure. Not being able to drive the car, stay out past eleven, or do everything their friends do isn't pressure.

The reason we consider that pressure is because we've magnified it. "Peer acceptance is so important. You need to feel good about yourself and have positive self-esteem." A hundred and fifty years ago people were just trying to survive and live another day. They didn't have time to think about their self-esteem. The reason so many people are so messed up emotionally today is because we have misplaced values.

"But we live in a high-stress society. Nobody has lived under the pressure we have today." Have you ever been a soldier in a combat zone? That's pressure. Wives and children during World War II had to see their husbands and fathers go off to war and never come back. That's pressure. Sitting in a traffic jam is only pressure because you make it pressure. It's because of the way you think. You needed five minutes to get from A to B, but you only gave yourself three. You put pressure on yourself and magnified these things.

This isn't a pressure society. It's the most privileged, luxurious, easy generation that's ever lived on the face of the earth. If you're feeling pressure, worn out, and burned out, it's because you have misplaced values. You're pressing yourself. It's not our society. You chose to get on the treadmill. You're the one who magnifies or minimizes everything that comes into your life.

"No Problem!"

A young minister and his wife were recently married. She told everyone that she wanted a dozen children. While they were out itinerating, she became pregnant. She called back and told everyone about it. They rejoiced with her. But when she returned and went to the doctor, they said it was a cancer and needed to do an immediate hysterectomy. The doctor told her she only had a 50 percent chance of living, and she couldn't live more than two weeks without the surgery. This woman was just devastated.

After a Thursday night service, I was laughing, joking, and cutting up with someone. This woman came over and tapped me on the shoulder. When I turned around, she was crying and asked, "Andrew, have you heard what they said?" I don't always respond this way, but I believe it was God that time. I just started laughing and declared, "Cancer's no problem with God. You act like all the lights in heaven would dim from the power drain if the Lord were to heal you, but it's not hard for God to heal cancer. No problem!"

It seemed as if I had slapped this woman in the face. She immediately stopped crying and asked, "Would you come over to our house and tell my husband and me about this?" So Jamie and I went over and talked to her. She said, "Well, what should I do?"

"It's your choice. You can pray and believe that the doctors will be blessed if you let them do the hysterectomy. You can go that route if you want to, but you'll never have children again."

"What other option do I have?"

"You can just believe God. It's not any harder to be healed of cancer than it is a cold."

She asked, "Do you really believe that?" So I started magnifying and glorifying God. I made the Lord bigger and diminished cancer. The only thing that makes cancer hard is the value you place on it.

She decided to believe God. So the doctors came and made her sign all this paperwork to absolve them of liability and responsibility "when" she died. They intimidated her and told her she was foolish. They tried to make her put more value on their diagnosis than God's Word.

Now, I'm not against doctors. I have one on my board of directors. Praise God for doctors. If it weren't for them, many Christians would have died prematurely. However, medical professionals are limited to the natural realm and they don't often value God, His Word, or His power.

These doctors tried to get her to change the value she had placed on God's ability. By His grace, she stood her ground. It's now been almost twenty years since she refused that operation—and she has a whole slew of children. Since no doctor would ever deliver her kids after seeing her records, she just had them all at home. It was that simple.

What's Bigger to You?

What do you value? What's big to you? Is cancer bigger to you than God? You can magnify the Lord and make Him bigger. The way you do it is by glorifying, praising, and thanking Him. Find someone in the Word who had a similar situation and overcame it. Meditate on and make these things more real to you than what your bank account, relatives, friends, or even what your own mind says. You need to get to a place where God's Word is true and the Lord is far bigger than the situation.

Consider Jehoshaphat going out and fighting the mighty armies arrayed against him. (2 Chron. 20.) He put the singers out in front of his army, praising the Lord, and God defeated the enemy without Jehoshaphat's men even drawing a sword or firing an arrow. Just say, "God, that's how big You are. You destroyed hundreds of thousands of enemy troops through singers praising You. You're awesome!" That makes God bigger. Then you intentionally disesteem your problems and say, "This is of no value. It's of no worth to me."

I'm not in the ministry to have you like me. I'm doing it because God has placed a call on my life. When He called me, I was an introvert. I was shy, embarrassed, and could hardly talk to anyone. Standing in front of people was the last thing I wanted to do, and for the first two years, it was terrible. I struggled with fear and all kinds of things. But the Lord has shared some truths with me that have changed both my life and many others. So I minister out of love for God and to help people. However, I don't prefer that you dislike me.

It doesn't bless me when someone comes up after a service and tells me they didn't like the message. But do you know what? It doesn't keep me up at night either. I don't lose one bit of sleep over it. Why? When it comes right down to it, I don't give a rip. I minister because I value God so much and He's leading me to do it—whether anyone likes what I have to say or not.

If you're afraid to witness, it's because you value the opinion and acceptance of others more than God's in your life. You don't want to expose yourself to the possibility of someone ridiculing, criticizing, or otherwise rejecting you. You haven't placed a proper value on God.

Refreshed and Restored

All Satan has to do after the Lord moves in your life is to put you in a situation where you compromise in some way or another. You have all these other things that are so important to you that you have to maintain, so you walk away from the revelation of God. But the Lord never quits transmitting.

God's love, joy, peace, healing, anointing, presence—or anything else—is there for you the same as the moment you experienced Him. God loves you the same now as He did then. In fact, He loves you more than you've ever yet perceived—ever! God isn't the variable. You disesteemed God when you started esteeming someone or something else.

However, you can go back and refresh those things in your life by glorifying God. Say, "Father, forgive me for placing such value on other things. Forgive me for letting what other people thought be more important than what You've said and done. Forgive me for being more interested in the Super Bowl and the World Series than You. Forgive me for magnifying my business, family, and other things above You. I put them ahead of You and forgot You."

The way you glorify God is by talking about Him. Remember what He's said and done. Be thankful, and as you magnify the Lord, what He's done in your life will be refreshed and restored.

I constantly go back and remember the things that God has done in my life. They're actually more real to me now than when they first happened. They're bigger in my life today than they were over thirty-five years ago. I've never had to return to my first love because I've never left. (Rev. 2:4.)

If you have, don't be condemned. Just return to Him. But don't ask God for a "fresh outpouring" of His love. That's like saying, "Lord, what You did wasn't good enough." God never quit transmitting. It was you who stopped receiving. Come back to Him and say, "Father, forgive me for ever walking away from what You said and did in my life. I valued, prized, and esteemed other things more highly than You." You can go right back to wherever you left God, and start putting the proper worth, value, and esteem on Him. You can recover anything that you've lost.

Encourage Yourself

The truth is—you never lost it. If you were ever healed, His healing virtue is still in you. It never leaves. (Rom. 11:29.) God never stopped releasing, but you quit receiving. Go back and build yourself up in that area. Receive by faith what the Lord has already provided by grace.

> David encouraged himself in the LORD his God.
>
> 1 SAMUEL 30:6

In the midst of David's darkest moment, he magnified God. His troops spoke of stoning him. All their beloved wives and children were gone—not to mention their possessions. But instead of becoming discouraged and thinking, *Poor old me,* David encouraged himself in the Lord. He began to glorify and magnify God in the midst of a bad situation.

You can do that too. You can choose to get down, bawl and squall, gripe and complain. Or you can choose to magnify and glorify God.

I haven't been discouraged and depressed since 1968. "But Andrew, you must not have any problems." I have problems just like anybody. In fact, ministers have more problems than others because we have invisible targets on us in the spirit realm. However, I've made some conscious decisions that I like being full of joy and peace more than I like being discouraged and depressed. So I just encourage myself in the Lord.

Sometimes I have to literally shut out what's going on in my life and force myself to focus on God. I have to turn away from looking at the natural circumstances and choose to magnify and glorify God. At times, I've had to start doing it through gritted teeth. I didn't feel like it. I didn't have a rush of positive emotion. But through clenched teeth I said, "God, I glorify You. You are awesome!" It wasn't very long before the joy and peace started flowing.

Raised from the Dead

Jamie and I received a call at 4:15 in the morning on March 4, 2001. It was our oldest son, Joshua, who told us that our youngest son, Peter, was dead. He'd been dead for over four hours. We had negative emotions just like you would've had, but—like I've been teaching in this book—I refused to let grief and sorrow occupy a higher place than my praise of God.

As Jamie and I drove that hour into town, I just started praising God. I thanked Him for His faithfulness and let Him know that I would continue serving and loving Him with all my heart regardless of what happened with our son.

As I began to magnify God, faith rose up in my heart and I knew that I knew Peter would live. When we arrived in Colorado Springs, we found out that five or ten minutes after we had received the call, Peter just sat up and started talking. He'd been stripped naked and put in a cooler with a toe tag on him, but God raised him from the dead after nearly five hours. Thank You, Jesus! And there was no brain damage—or as Peter himself said—"No more brain damage than before."

All of this happened because I refused to let anything else occupy God's rightful place.

You're the one who can choose to do these things. You can edify yourself.

Give Glory

Abraham "was strong in faith, [how?] giving glory to God" (Rom. 4:20).

Magnify God. Give Him glory. Put worth and value on Him. Say, "Lord, You're bigger than this financial problem, marriage issue, relationship challenge, health crisis, or job. God, You're bigger than anything. You are awesome!" When you start magnifying God, your faith just grows.

The reason some of us don't operate in more faith is that we haven't spent any time magnifying God and verbally acknowledging He's bigger than our problem. You need to say things like, "God, You are bigger than my problem. You're bigger than these situations I'm facing." When you magnify and glorify Him, your faith rises and anything is possible.

All things *are* possible to him that believeth.

MARK 9:23

But it's up to you to glorify God.

God Matters Most

A lot of Christians aren't doing this very well today. We magnify our problems. Our society is geared toward magnifying insignificant things. Therefore, we need to put the right value on things.

One night, someone broke into a department store and didn't steal anything, but they did change all the price tags around. The next day, a $200 vacuum cleaner sold for $8, and an $8 item sold for $200. That store did business until noon before they figured out what had happened. This caused great havoc!

That's what Satan has done in our society. He's come in and changed the value on us. We think we need certain things. We put so much attention on physical, material things, but they don't really matter in light of eternity. When it's all over, God is who will matter most.

Your relationship with the Lord is really the only thing that matters in your life. For that reason you need to place value and worth upon it. Do so consistently and you'll stay full of healing, joy, peace, deliverance, anointing, power—whatever you need. You are the one who determines how full you are. God isn't the One who decides. True revival is simply you becoming so full of God that you overflow onto someone else. This isn't up to God—it's up to you.

CHAPTER 5

Set Joy Before You

Most Christians don't know how to maintain what God has done for them. He touches their lives and they get turned on to Him, but six months later it's as if they've lost the passion to know and serve Him. This isn't the way God intended it to be.

Romans 1:21 shows us how people walk away from a revelation of God's existence, His hatred for sin, and how we're accountable to Him. It reveals four things we do to harden and desensitize ourselves to what God has done in our lives.

First, we don't glorify God. We don't put value and worth on Him. We don't esteem—prize—the revelation He gives us. The word *glorify* speaks of the value we place on what God has said and done.

Most people don't value the things of God properly. When we begin valuing the opinions and experiences of others more than what God says in His Word and how He's touched our life, we begin to be insensitive. The blessing, benefit, and joy of what God has done for us starts wearing off when we quit placing the proper value on it.

Look Past the Heartache

Not only do you need to put a positive value on what God has said and done in your life, but you also need to devalue anything else that comes against you. It's a two-edged sword!

You can't just say, "Father, I value what You've done. I glorify You and magnify what You've done in my life." You also have to make a conscious effort to disesteem and devalue everything else in a comparative sense.

Jesus faced the cross, but focused on "the joy that was set before Him" (Heb. 12:2). Mentally, He captured His thoughts. It wasn't natural. As He headed to the cross, Jesus didn't just have a rush of natural feelings, like excitement and happiness. It took effort, but He looked beyond the cross and saw the joy there.

He saw the fact that this would please His Father, appease His wrath, and that He would resurrect from the dead and one day be seated at the Father's right hand. He also saw you and me. The Lord's heart beat with such love for the world that it enabled Him to look past the heartache.

Minimize the Negative

This is such an important key to victory. If you ever do anything that amounts to anything, if you ever touch someone else's life, if you ever succeed in any endeavor, there will be problems between you and that success. The person who succeeds is the one who can look past those problems, hurts, pains, and actually glorify, magnify, and esteem the solution. They can see beyond the cost and value the answer above it. That's what separates losers and victors.

Every millionaire I've ever read about has gone bust more than once, but they had something on the inside that just kept them moving forward anyway. They knew that they knew that they knew that there was a way to succeed. So they kept this goal—this prize—in front of them. Because of it, they were able to take things that destroyed other people.

I've also seen just the opposite. Even though everything seems to work for some people, they just have a defeated mentality and expect something to fail. Then they fall apart like a two-dollar suitcase when the first little problem comes their way. The issue isn't the challenging situation on the outside, but the failure on the inside.

The Lord set the joy in front of Him and despised—disesteemed—the shame. (Heb. 12:2.) Your thoughts either magnify or shrink everything. It's not what happens to you that's important, but how you perceive and process it.

When you magnify negative things, they become insurmountable. But you can also take huge things and disesteem—shrink—them. If Jesus could take the cross and the shame associated with it and disesteem it, then you can despise anything. You can reduce anything that comes against you to nothing.

All Times!

I will bless the LORD at all times: his praise *shall* continually *be* in my mouth.

PSALM 34:1

Most Christians know this scripture, but don't really believe it works. They say, "Well, you can praise God up to a point, but beyond that you can't expect me to praise the Lord in this situation." In other words, the Word doesn't really mean "all times." It means all times except "these times."

If you put the proper value and worth on God and spiritual things, nothing in this life can compare. You can disesteem and devalue anything in this life so that nothing can bother you or steal your joy.

"But what if you're going through a divorce? What if your spouse cheated on you? It's terrible! How can you rejoice through that? Psychology would say that you're in denial."

You could focus on the Lord and say, "Thank You, Jesus, that Your Word says that in heaven we won't marry or be given in marriage. (Matt. 22:30.) This is temporary. I'm so glad I get to live forever with You and not this other person." Now that's something to rejoice about! "Thank You, Jesus, that You'll never divorce me. You'll never leave me nor forsake me." (Heb. 13:5.) You can rejoice even if you're going through a divorce.

Change Your World

Who cares if you're going to die? You're going to die someday anyway. Life is a terminal experience. We're all in different stages of dying—even younger folks. You don't have as many years left as you used to. "Oh, that's terrible!" Paul didn't think so. He wrestled between his strong desire to go be with the Lord and staying here to minister.

If you value things properly, you can get to a place where dying isn't a problem. When the doctor tells you you're going to die, you could just reach up and kiss him saying, "That's awesome! I believe in healing, so I believe God will heal me. But if I'm not healed, it'll be awesome just to sit in the presence of the Lord. What a deal!"

If you can't do that, it's because you have misplaced values. You still glorify this physical life—carnal things—more than eternal things.

Marriage is wonderful. Praise God for marriage. But if your marriage is so important that you couldn't make it without your mate, you have misplaced values. If your marriage went south all of a sudden and you couldn't survive, you have wrong values.

John Wesley—the great revivalist—had a horrible marriage. I've been to his house in London. His wife used to kick him and hit him while he was praying. She hated both God and him, yet he lived with her for twenty years. Even though she beat him, Wesley just went on and changed the world for God.

Responsive to God

"But my spouse doesn't love and appreciate me. It's stunting my growth." Pull your thumb out of your mouth and grow up. Recognize that there's something bigger than that. Just go on and follow the Lord.

Jesus faced the cross and counted it as nothing compared to the joy He focused on. He was stripped naked, spit on, beard plucked out, thorns in His brow, back shredded, and ridiculed, but He disesteemed all that. It didn't matter. He was thinking on the joy to come.

Most of what we worry about is so insignificant. Some people say, "When I get to heaven, I'm going to ask God about this and that." No, you won't. Once you get there and know all things as you are known, you'll see everything in its right perspective. In view of God's awesomeness and splendor, you'll say, "I'm sure glad I didn't ask that stupid question and air out my little gripe." When you find yourself standing before Almighty God, you won't be holding Him to account saying, "Why didn't You do this and why didn't You do that?" Once you get God's perspective, it'll change your life.

The reason things are so big to us is that God is so small to us. If you would exalt, magnify, and value the Lord properly, He would become so big to you that all this other stuff wouldn't even matter. It wouldn't even be important. Once you get that attitude, you'll find that everything else in the natural will work better for you. You'll receive your healing easier. Your finances will work better. Your marriage will improve because you aren't codependent upon that person anymore. If they do something wrong, it won't affect your walk. You'll just keep right on walking with God, which is the best thing you can do for your mate anyhow.

My wife knows that I love God more than her—and vice versa. That would hurt and bother some people, but it's a blessing to me. Why? There are times when I do things wrong and disappoint my wife. If she gave me what I deserved, then I'd be in trouble. But Jamie has a commitment to the Lord and I know He's never wrong. God is always the same. He's the One who brought us together in the first place, and He's the One who wants our marriage to stay together. I take great pleasure in the fact that my wife is more responsive to God than she is to me.

Perspective

Jesus set this joy before Himself, and that allowed Him to endure the cross. If you aren't enduring, it's probably because you don't have any joy set before you that you're focusing on instead. You're like a fly on a painting. Flies have compound eyes and see a thousand images of everything. Right now, you see 2,000 blobs of this ugly red color. But if you backed up and viewed the picture in perspective, you'd see how that little blob of paint fits perfectly and helps make it a masterpiece.

You can get so close to your problem that you can't see anything else and you think the whole world is falling apart because of it. You need to get focused on something other than what's going on right now. Look beyond it. Lift your eyes up and look somewhere other than just down at your feet and what's going on.

Jesus overlooked His problem. That's what enabled Him to endure it. He disesteemed the shame and focused on the joy—and you can too.

CHAPTER 6

It's Always Better to Choose God

By faith Moses, when he was come to years, refused to be called the son of Pharaoh's daughter; choosing rather to suffer affliction with the people of God, than to enjoy the pleasures of sin for a season; *esteeming* the reproach of Christ greater riches than the treasures in Egypt: for he had *respect* unto the recompence of the reward.

HEBREWS 11:24-26

Moses esteemed suffering, rejection, and persecution as being more valuable than all the treasures of Egypt. This was no small deal. He was second in command of the world superpower of his day. Secular history records that Moses went out and defeated the Ethiopians. He was a general who held a great position of authority, but he esteemed God's will above all this wealth and power.

What Do You Respect?

If you were put in that position, it'd be a struggle for you to identify with the slaves. If God said, "These Egyptians you grew up with aren't really your people," you'd probably struggle. Why? Because you'd say, "Oh Lord, look what I'd be giving up!" The reason you sometimes struggle to do God's will is because of the value you place on other things.

Moses was able to do it because he determined in his heart that, "Doing God's will means much more to me than losing the throne. Suffering with Christ and giving up this power and wealth pales in comparison to my reward. Even if I have to go out into the wilderness for forty years, He's worth more. Fulfilling my God-given destiny is more valuable to me than all that Egypt could offer." That's the reason he could do it.

Sometimes we look at people who have made great sacrifices and wonder, *How could they do it?* Well, they couldn't with some people's values! People generally will do what they value, prize, and respect the most. Therefore, the problem isn't knowing what the right thing to do is. It's that our values are so skewed that we can't make the right decision to do it because we feel we're losing so much.

It appeared as if Moses was losing everything, but he looked beyond that. He had "respect" unto his reward. (Heb.

11:26.) *Respect* means "to turn the eyes away from other things and fix them on some one thing."[1]Moses looked away from everything but his reward. In other words, he refused to sit down, count, and dwell on all the different things he was giving up. He turned away from everything and became single-minded on what God had promised him. If he hadn't, you probably never would have heard of Moses.

Choosing God always, always, always works out to your best interests. It looked like Moses was giving up a lot, but he chose God and changed the course of the entire world. There isn't a Christian on the planet today who hasn't heard the name of Moses. Most secular, Jewish, and Muslim people have heard his name too. Almost everybody has heard of Moses! But no one would have heard of him in this day and age if he had chosen the riches of Egypt instead. Moses made the better choice. When you choose God's way, it'll always work out better for you in the end. But the problem is we say, "Lord, if I do what You're asking me to do, I'll have to give up this and that!"

"No Way!"

After returning home from Vietnam, I started working in a film department in the public school system. Even though I was a college dropout, I gave that job everything I had. I developed and edited films, and delivered them to the schools. That's what I did, but I did it as unto the Lord. I prayed over my work and gave it my best shot.

Within a few months, the head of the entire department came to me and said, "I really like you and the work you do, so I'm going to offer you a job. You could work here for thirty-five years and retire. This job includes guaranteed retirement. The catch is you have to have a minimum of five years commitment." He wanted to put me into a management position when I was just twenty years old!

This was a great opportunity, especially for a college dropout. However, it was right at the time when the Lord had told me I was supposed to go into the ministry. So I decided, "No way!" Even though I didn't know much of God's plan for my life yet, I valued it more. At the time, this was a real temptation for me. But I look back now and say, "Thank You, Jesus, that I didn't choose that job editing film!"

What God has done in my life is so much greater than that. It's so much more awesome. I never would have gotten out of town had I done that. But I get to travel the world and minister to all kinds of different people. What a privilege!

It's always better to choose God. You just need to change your value system and disesteem everything else. Get to a place where you look away from anything except the Lord. Say, "Father, You are all I want. Your will is all I need in my life."

Paul Counted

Paul considered everything he had as worthless compared to knowing God. He wasn't talking about all of his failures and the things he did wrong. Paul was referring to all of his education, degrees, and accomplishments. Paul was probably one of the most educated men of his day. He was the up and coming rabbi in the nation of Israel. He had all these things going for him in the natural.

> But what things were gain to me, those I *counted* loss for Christ. Yea doubtless, and I *count* all things *but* loss for the excellency of the knowledge of Christ Jesus my Lord: for whom I have suffered the loss of all things, and do *count* them *but* dung, that I may win Christ.
>
> PHILIPPIANS 3:7,8

"Count"[2]here is the same Greek word used in Hebrews 11:26 for "esteeming,"[3]where the Bible says that Moses esteemed the persecution that came with serving God as greater riches than all of Egypt's treasures.

Paul valued God and disesteemed everything else. The worth he placed on all of his education and accomplishments was equal to dung. Do you know what we do with our dung? We frame it and put it on the wall.

"Jesus, You're It!"

If you truly counted everything except the knowledge of Christ as dung, then you'd be like Paul when people come and say, "We're going to kill you!"

He answered, "Wonderful! Kill me. I'll go be with God."

However, very few of us would react that way. Why? We haven't yet counted everything but the intimate, experiential knowledge of Christ as dung.

You really do value your reputation and all those material possessions you have. I'm not saying that you shouldn't value them at all. It's just comparatively their relative worth ought to pale in light of the high value you place on the Lord and His power in your life. If someone pointed a gun at your head and said, "Choose between your life and God right now," it'd be no choice. "Jesus, You're it. I'd die for You in a heartbeat." You might think you can't do that, but you can.

Every person in the Bible who ever did anything glorified God. They put more value and worth on what He said and His plan for their life. They simply loved God more than they loved themselves. That's the key.

You'll Love It

You need to get to the place where you value the things of God more than you value your things. When the Lord is worth more to you than even your own life, then the Christian life becomes easy.

Most people believe that God will make you do something you don't want to do. "The Lord might send me to the deepest corner of Africa." God isn't going to do something to hurt you. That's not how He works at all.

> Delight thyself also in the LORD; and he shall give thee the desires of thine heart.
>
> PSALM 37:4

This doesn't mean that He'll just give you anything you want. It means that God will put His desires in your heart. When you're delighting yourself in the Lord—when you're valuing and esteeming Him more than anything else—you can do what you want to. Why? Because your want-tos will change. If the Lord wants to send you to the deepest corner of Africa—and you've been delighting yourself in Him—you won't be happy anywhere else. You'll love it!

A couple of my friends are missionaries to Mexico. They've lived there over twenty years now. They can't even conceive moving back to the States. They love it down there because that's where God has called them to be.

CHAPTER 7

Thankfulness Glorifies God

The second key to staying full of God is to avoid doing this:

Neither were thankful.

ROMANS 1:21

In Chapter 4, we saw that to magnify God is to glorify Him. In light of this truth, consider this verse in Psalm 69:

I will praise the name of God with a song, and will magnify him with thanksgiving.

PSALM 69:30

Glorifying, magnifying, and thanking God are all interrelated and intertwined. In order to glorify God, you need to be thankful. As you are thanking Him, you're reminding yourself of what He has said and done, which magnifies Him. As you think on the Lord in this way, He becomes bigger and more powerful in your life. In order to truly magnify and glorify God, you must be thankful for what He's done.

Memory and Humility

Unthankfulness is one of the blights of our generation.

> In the last days perilous times shall come. For men shall be lovers of their own selves, covetous, boasters, proud, blasphemers, disobedient to parents, *unthankful,* unholy…lovers of pleasures more than lovers of God.
>
> 2 TIMOTHY 3:1,2,4

Being unthankful is listed right there next to being unholy. It's mentioned in the same list as blasphemers and lovers of pleasure more than God. Does that describe our society or what! Huge amounts of the population today are unthankful. They simply don't remember or acknowledge the goodness of God.

Being thankful involves memory and humility. You can't be thankful without remembering the good things that have been done for you. A proud person doesn't believe anyone else has helped them do anything. They've accomplished everything "on their own." They don't acknowledge the contribution and help of anyone or anything else. This attitude of "I'm a self-made man (or woman)" is just rampant today. Very few people remember.

Bless the LORD, O my soul, and forget not all his benefits.

PSALM 103:2

God commanded you not to forget because He knows you will if you don't make a decision to remember. That's why the Lord instituted the different observances in the Bible like communion, Passover, and other special feasts. This was also why they made memorial markers and piles of stones. It was to stir the people up through memory.

You Can't Function Without Memory

Your memory is one of the most powerful faculties you have.

A couple of weeks after their wedding, a man and his wife were in a car wreck. The woman was driving and the man was asleep in the back seat. He survived relatively unhurt, but she almost died. Although she pulled through and recovered, she lost the last twelve months of her memory. She remembered her parents, her name, and everything about herself up to a year before the accident, but everything after that was gone.

Those previous twelve months had been when she met, fell in love with, and married this man. Although she didn't remember him, everyone told her that this guy was her husband. She went home with him, but didn't remember him. They tried to have a physical relationship, but she just couldn't handle it. Finally, they had to break up, move out, and start courting again because she couldn't maintain the relationship without her memory.

If you couldn't remember, just think what it would do to your life. What would it do to your marriage, children, work, and church situation? You can't function without memory, and yet, very few people remember the goodness of God.

Never Forget!

In order to maintain the things that God does in your life, you're going to have to be one thankful person. You need to constantly go back and rehearse your victories and the encounters you've had with Him.

For some Christians, every day is a brand-new day with no history. When they get up in the morning, they aren't sure whether or not they'll still be serving God by that night. It just depends on how things go during the day. They don't want to go out and disown God, they desire to remain faithful, but they can't guarantee that they will. God forbid they get put in a compromising situation because they just don't know for sure what they're going to do.

My life is the exact opposite. I can truthfully say that nearly every day since March 23, 1968, I've remembered what God has done in my life. I'm one thankful guy! I thank the Lord constantly. I stir myself up to remember when God touched my life and I've never forgotten it.

Remember the Pit

> Hearken to me, ye that follow after righteousness, ye that seek the LORD: look unto the rock *whence* ye are hewn, and to the hole of the pit *whence* ye are digged.
>
> ISAIAH 51:1

At the same time you're looking at the Lord and seeing your position in Him, you must also remember the pit you crawled out of. If you did, it would change the way you act. If I woke up one morning and Satan put pressure on me to renounce God, I couldn't do it. Why? I have a history. I have nearly five decades worth of being born again and forty years of wholeheartedly seeking God interwoven into my thoughts and life. If someone came up to me and tried to get me to deny the Lord, I couldn't. He's been such an important part of my life for so long now. But there are some folks who wake up each morning having forgotten everything the Lord has done for them.

I remember where I was when God touched my life. It was so dramatic and so important that nothing compares to it. There's nothing that could tempt me to ever turn away from God. I recognize that I'm capable of doing anything that anybody else is capable of, but not today. My heart is fixed on God and I'm rehearsing my victories. I'm glorifying and thanking God!

I don't know how long it would take me—six months, a year, two years, three years of denying God—to let these memories and this passion for the Lord fade. I could eventually do something, but not today. You can't make me turn on God and commit adultery today because I love Him and I'm remembering what He has done.

Are you glorifying, remembering, and being thankful for what God has already done in your life? Or are you just driving down the street hoping that the devil doesn't put a temptation in your path because you don't know if you'll make it? There's something powerful about going back, rehearsing your victories, and being thankful.

CHAPTER 8

Stirred Up by Memory

Memory is such a powerful force, Peter referred to it three times in his second letter:

> Wherefore I will not be negligent *to put you always in remembrance of these things,* though ye know *them,* and be established in the present truth. Yea, I think it meet, as long as I am in this tabernacle, *to stir you up by putting you in remembrance.*
>
> 2 PETER 1:12,13

> Moreover I will endeavour that ye may be able after my decease *to have these things always in remembrance.*
>
> 2 PETER 1:15

> This second epistle, beloved, I now write unto you; in *both* which I stir up your pure minds by way of remembrance.
>
> 2 PETER 3:1

If you don't stir yourself up, you'll settle to the bottom. Therefore, go back and remember. I bet God has saved your bacon more than once. If you would just sit down and spend some time thinking about how the Lord has been good to you, your entire outlook would change for the better. If you're wondering, *God, where are You? Do You love me?* just go back and think about the awesome things the Lord has done for you.

He Preserves the Simple

Some pastors and I were joking and sharing experiences with each other in Florida. I told them about the time I rode in a tiny little airplane with this one guy. The plane was so small, his shoulder touched the window, my shoulder touched the window, and our two other shoulders touched in between. That plane was going up and down like a roller coaster, dropping a thousand feet at a time, and flying nearly sideways. It was a mess.

This "pilot" finally threw his hands up over his eyes and screamed, "My God, we're going to die! We're going to die!" Then he just rolled up into a ball—and there I was with him in this airplane. So I flew it with one hand and shook him with the other, saying, "God didn't let me live through Vietnam to die in your plane!" I had to fly that thing for over an hour.

We flew over Alamogordo Rifle Range. They came on the radio and said they were going to shoot us down. I told them, "Hey, the pilot has freaked! Have mercy on me. I'm getting out of here just as fast as I can." I never heard from the tower again. They were probably laughing too hard to speak!

On another occasion, a three-foot tall boulder that weighed close to a ton rolled over my arm and head. I immediately jumped up, started shouting the name of Jesus and screaming, "I'm healed! I'm healed!" About thirty seconds later, I stopped, looked, and everything worked. Praise God! So I erected a monument there that says, "August 25, 1999. Jesus saved my life when this rock rolled over my hand, arm, and head. Psalm 116:6." That verse says:

> The LORD preserveth the simple: I was brought low, and he helped me.

Every time I walk by that spot on our property, I see it and thank God.

Escapes from Death

As these pastors and I were sharing our stories, I recounted over thirty different times where I should have been dead. I remembered when my brother picked me up off the bottom of a hotel swimming pool at eleven o'clock at night. I'd been knocked out when I hit my head on the diving board while trying to do a flip. My brother saw what happened and saved my life. On another occasion, I fell off a thousand-foot cliff and my brother caught me in mid-air. As I remembered these things, I was deeply moved.

I told the Lord, "Father, You have a purpose for my life and You aren't through with me yet. There's a reason for me being alive today—praise Your awesome name." Even though it's been more than a year since these pastors and I had this conversation, I've been overwhelmed thinking about God's goodness and grace in my life ever since.

> *He that is* our God *is* the God of salvation; and unto GOD the Lord *belong* the issues [escapes[1]] from death.
>
> PSALM 68:20

I bet God has saved your life many times, but you have forgotten. Now that I've jogged your memory, it's coming back to you. If you would just rehearse those victories and think about God's goodness, you wouldn't get halfway through before someone would have to scrape you off the ceiling. Discouragement would just leave.

If you're depressed, you haven't been thinking about what God has done for you. Instead, you're thinking on what the devil is doing to you. You aren't focusing on the joy that is set before you. You aren't saying, "If I die, I'll go to be with the Lord. If I'm poor, I have a mansion in heaven on streets of gold." You're just looking at your present situation. You can't be depressed without first getting your eyes off Jesus and what He's done, forgetting His goodness in the past, and forgetting the goodness of the future He's promised you. You just forget everything.

If you want to be depressed, there are plenty of depressing things you can think on. But if you look at things properly, are thankful, and remember, you have no reason to be discouraged. You'll get this attitude that says, "It doesn't matter what's happening on the outside, God in me is bigger and stronger!"

The Vacuum Within

I remember a science experiment my sixth-grade teacher did. He put a little one-gallon metal gas can on a Bunsen burner and heated it. Then as soon as it became hot, he put the cap back on real tight. He set that can on his desk and just kept on teaching. As the air cooled, it formed a vacuum on the inside of that can. Since I was sitting there in the front row, I can vividly remember watching that can. It started crackling and popping without anyone touching it. Then—all of a sudden—it became crushed. It looked to me like someone had taken a sledgehammer to it. That can just fell to the ground and continued getting crushed. I watched the entire scenario. Nobody touched it. This was just natural atmospheric pressure acting on a can with nothing inside.

It's the vacuum within—not the pressure without—that's causing people to be crushed today. Under normal circumstances, the pressure within would have enabled the can to have no problem withstanding the pressures without. However, the absence of pressure within caused normal atmospheric pressure to crush it. Some people just can't handle the pressure in their marriage. They love talking about how bad it is, putting great value on these pressures and saying, "Nobody knows the trouble I feel. Nobody knows my sorrow." Then they sing these songs about how "Nobody has as much trouble as I do" and it makes them feel justified.

As long as the devil can make you feel like nobody else has ever had your situation, it doesn't matter. I could preach my heart out and tell you everything I know, but you'd still just sit there saying, "That's true, but it won't work for me."

> There hath no temptation taken you but such as is common to man.
>
> 1 CORINTHIANS 10:13

The temptations you face are common to everyone. We all have the same problems. It may be packaged in a different wrapper, but it's the same contents. The devil doesn't have a bunch of different tricks. He just has a few that he rewraps and uses on all of us. But the moment you say, "I'm the only one," you've fallen for a lie and exempted yourself from the answer.

You don't have any pressure that's beyond God's ability. It's your vacuum within that's the problem. It's the fact that you aren't glorifying God, rehearsing your victories, or being thankful. You aren't using your mind to remember what God has said and done.

Be Thankful

If you remembered God, your situation wouldn't seem so bad. Remember when you were born again. What was it the Lord saved you out of? Remember the joy and peace that flooded your entire being. What vision has He placed in your heart? What words has He spoken to you? Remind yourself, then:

> Enter into his gates with thanksgiving, *and* into his courts with praise: be thankful unto him, *and* bless his name. For the LORD *is* good; his mercy *is* everlasting; and his truth *endureth* to all generations.
>
> PSALM 100:4,5

Even if you think your situation is so bad that you need to gripe and complain, enter into His gates with thanksgiving and His courts with praise. For every five minutes you spend whining, spend another ten minutes thanking God for His goodness. If you do that, you'll find that your gripe will have shrunk really small by the time you get around to it. Then you'll look at that thing and say, "It's no big deal."

I've seen people who were miraculously healed of incurable diseases come down with a cold. It's dragged on and they've had trouble getting their faith to work. So they've come to me and said, "If God can't heal me of this cold, I'm going to quit." That's when the spirit of slap comes all over me. I just want to whack them upside the head and say, "Don't you remember what God did? You've already been healed, but you forgot. Now you have everything way out of perspective."

No one has a right to gripe and complain. Nobody will stand before the Lord and say, "God, You let me down." Don't grow weary and faint. Maintain your faith and enthusiasm. Be a good receiver.

Light Affliction

For which cause we faint not; but though our outward man perish, yet the inward *man* is renewed day by day.

2 CORINTHIANS 4:16

Paul wasn't saying that he didn't have problems. He said, "Outwardly I perish. All of these circumstances and situations keep happening to me all the time. But—my inward man is renewed day by day."

> For our light affliction, which is but for a moment.
>
> 2 CORINTHIANS 4:17

Many people think, "Well, Paul's affliction was light. Mine is heavy. So I can't relate to or accept what you're saying."

Paul experienced some extremely harsh situations. Let's take a look at some of Paul's "light" afflictions.

> In labours more abundant, in stripes above measure, in prisons more frequent, in deaths oft. Of the Jews five times received I forty *stripes* save one. Thrice was I beaten with rods, once was I stoned, thrice I suffered shipwreck, a night and a day I have been in the deep; *in* journeyings often, *in* perils of waters, *in* perils of robbers, *in* perils by *mine own* countrymen, *in* perils by the heathen, *in* perils in the city, *in* perils in the wilderness, *in* perils in the sea, *in* perils among false brethren; in weariness and painfulness, in watchings often, in hunger and thirst, in fastings often, in cold and nakedness. Beside those things that are without, that which cometh upon me daily, the care of all the churches.
>
> 2 CORINTHIANS 11:23-28

No Right to Complain

And there came thither *certain* Jews from Antioch and Iconium, who persuaded the people, and, having stoned Paul, drew *him* out of the city, supposing he had been dead. Howbeit, as the disciples stood round about him, he rose up, and came into the city: and the next day he departed with Barnabas to Derbe.

ACTS 14:19,20

When the Jews stoned someone, they didn't stop until they were sure the person was dead. So it's very likely Paul was raised from the dead. These were just some of his "light" afflictions!

Paul's afflictions were much more in quantity and intensity than anything you've experienced. If he could say, "My afflictions were light," then you don't have any right to gripe and complain. Your problems don't even come close to what Paul went through.

Praise the Lord

After Hebrews 12:2 reveals that Jesus despised—disesteemed—the shame of the cross, God's Word continues, saying:

Consider him that endured...lest ye be wearied and faint in your minds. Ye have not yet resisted unto blood, striving against sin.

HEBREWS 12:3,4

Consider what Jesus suffered for you. Until you've suffered to the point that it costs you your life, you have no right to complain.

If you're alive, you ought to be praising God!

> Let every thing that hath breath praise the LORD.
>
> PSALM 150:6

You should be thanking God instead of griping and complaining.

"But Andrew, you don't know my situation." Wrong! You value things differently than God does. You really do value your problems, hurts, and pains. However, the truth is you don't have a right to complain. God's supply is far bigger than your need.

> For our light affliction, which is but for a moment.
>
> 2 CORINTHIANS 4:17

Your affliction is light because it's temporary. It's but for a moment. If you think everything in your life is bleak, you don't have a very good reference point. You're comparing yourself with your neighbors, or you're looking at the totally unrealistic picture of reality that's painted on television. If you're using those things as your standard, it'll create dissatisfaction on the inside of you. You need the proper perspective. Stir yourself up to remember what God has done.

CHAPTER 9

Remember His Goodness

Everyone has a reason to praise God. But if you think that your situation really is that pitiful, put it in its proper perspective and say, "Praise God, this is temporary!" Whether you are suffering physically, financially, emotionally, relationally—whatever it is—it's just temporary. After you've been in eternity for a billion years, you'll look back on this and think, *That wasn't so bad!* When you look at your circumstances in light of eternity, it changes your perspective.

> While we look not at the things which are seen, but at the things which are not seen: for the things which are seen *are* temporal; but the things which are not seen *are* eternal.
>
> 2 CORINTHIANS 4:18

If you're depressed, discouraged, and losing your joy, you aren't looking at the Lord and His Word. If the things of God aren't fresh in your life, then you aren't esteeming eternal reality. You're placing a higher value on the natural realm and magnifying physical things instead. That's where your discontent comes from.

Depression isn't caused by genes or hormones. It's not a chemical imbalance either. Chemical imbalances do happen, but it's a by-product of wrong thinking.[1]

One of our Bible college students was manic-depressive. One time he went off his medication and flipped out. This guy was headed to Mexico with us the next week, and he was believing God that he was healed. I told him, "Brother, I believe you're healed too, but we aren't going to let you run off and try to hurt someone in a foreign culture. You don't want to live in a Mexican prison. So we're going to believe God with you for your healing to manifest and as long as you're fine, we're with you. But if you start flipping out, you're going to have to take your medicine. Because we love you, we'll make sure you get the proper dosage to settle you down and we can bring you back here to the States."

This fellow's chemical imbalance wasn't causing his depression. It was his negativism and tendency to focus on the wrong thing.

Fix Your Mind

Your emotions affect your body. They'll cause wrinkles on your face and your hair to turn gray. Mary, the Queen of

Scots, was a redhead. However, fear caused her hair to become snow-white. Doctors try to find out what's happening in your physical body to give you some way around it, but your body is responding to you.

> For to be carnally minded *is* death....
>
> ROMANS 8:6

Carnal mindedness affects your body.

> ...but to be spiritually minded *is* life and peace.
>
> ROMANS 8:6

If you aren't experiencing life and peace, it's because of your carnal mind.

The Lord "wilt keep *him* in perfect peace, *whose* mind *is* stayed *on thee*:because he trusteth in thee" (Isa. 26:3).

Peace is related to your thoughts. Your emotions are related to your thoughts, not your hormones. If it were just your circumstances that dictated how you feel, then everyone who is in bad circumstances would always feel bad. But that's not so. Some folks are in much worse situations than you, but they're rejoicing and praising the Lord.

All of our problems are small in comparison to God and His eternal point of view. He isn't up there in heaven wringing His hands and saying, "Oh no, I don't know what to do!" He's not upset or worried. Our "problems" don't overwhelm God. They're nothing compared to what He's already done for us through His Son. We need to adopt God's attitude and start seeing things from His perspective through the Word.

Just be thankful and remember His goodness. Study God's dealings with the children of Israel, especially when they came out of Egypt and were on their way into the Promised Land. Psalm 106 recounts three different times how they forgot His mighty works and ended up falling into problems. (vv. 7,13,21.)

If you keep your mind fixed on the goodness of God, you can't fail. Remembering the Lord is powerful. If you constantly keep God on your mind, it'll change your entire life.

Guard Your Heart and Mind

This is so simple that you have to have somebody help you to misunderstand it. God didn't make it complicated. It's our lifestyle, society, and value system that have complicated things. We've elevated the things God despises. We give great honor to movie stars and musicians who glorify and magnify sin. Reporters delve into their lives and tell us everything they can about these "wonderful" people. God isn't impressed when they win Oscars and Academy Awards for portraying adultery, murder, lying, and stealing in their movies and music. He doesn't value things the way we do.

Heaven doesn't shut down on Super Bowl Sunday so that everyone can watch the game. It's really no big deal. Now, there's nothing wrong with you catching the Super Bowl. But if watching people run a little pigskin ball up and down a field, kicking and throwing it, and hurting other people is more important to you than going to church and learning about the things of God, then something is wrong with your thinking. If watching "your team" every week is of higher value to you than God, then you have some serious problems.

You can't react differently than your dominant thought. You are what you think, and if you're thinking of all these other things, it'll draw you in that direction. You have to go out of your way to guard your heart and mind. When everyone else is falling at these people's feet saying, "They're so awesome. Look at their wealth. And oh, they're so beautiful!" it'll take effort to say, "Father, I know that's not the way You view things. This isn't important to You." God sees wealth and beauty differently than we do.

This is especially important in ministry. I know people who would be dead today if I hadn't prayed for them. Others would be in hell right now if I hadn't shared the gospel with them. A mother recently wrote to me how one of her sons had received my materials in prison. He became born again and God totally turned his life around through my tapes. Although he's since died, this grateful woman told me how her son was finally happy for the first time in his entire life. When you hear good reports like that on a regular basis, it's tempting to change values and think, "God, I really did something. I'm somebody special!"

That's when it's important to remember. When I was in high school, I was the flunky of everything. I was so bashful and intimidated that I couldn't even look a person in the face and talk to them. I was terribly introverted and had nothing going for me. I was heading nowhere in a hurry.

"I Can't Handle It Anymore!"

Memory will help you keep your feet on the ground. It'll prevent you from reading your own press releases or fainting in the middle of the fight.

Don Francisco, a good friend of mine, told me that he stuttered as a child. His teacher made him stand up in front of the whole class once to read a poem. He spent forty-five minutes and only got two sentences out. Now he sings these powerfully anointed songs, words just flow out of him, and he gets great acclaim and praise. But Don remembers that it's God, and not him.

Bob Nichols is another good friend of mine. His daughter has been in a coma now for many years. She wasn't supposed to live. I was there when the doctors came in and said, "Brother Nichols, you know that she's dead. Take the tubes out." They did a tracheotomy and I went in and saw her. Normally 130 pounds, she was down to sixty. She didn't look like a person. I'd never seen anybody look that bad and still be alive. It took all the faith I had not to confess my unbelief in front of Bob and Joy.

When the doctors pressed Bob, he didn't get mad and blast them. He didn't stand up and yell. He just said, "No, that's not what we're believing for," and went right on. She's back home now, and actually stands up and walks with a walker. They say she's still in a coma. She doesn't talk, but she'll squeeze your hand. The lights are on—praise God! Although they're seeing progress, the Nichols have struggled under this longer than most people could endure.

While I was preaching this message at a ministers' conference and emphasizing how God is good and nobody has a right to gripe, Bob stood up on the front row and declared, "I've taken all I can take. I can't handle it anymore!" Then he took off running, jumping, and yelling, "Oh God, You're so good. I love You!" He just went wild praising God. Ruined the whole sermon. Lost the whole group. A man who has suffered much more than we have probably ever thought about was so thankful that he just couldn't handle it. He wound up falling on the floor praising, thanking, and worshiping God for His goodness. And some of us gripe and complain over the piddling little problems we have.

No Reason to Complain

We need to repent. We need to say, "Father, forgive me for my hard heart. Forgive me for looking at others and for accepting the average way everyone else accepts while trying to be just a little bit better. God, You are a good God. You have blessed me so much. Thank You!" If you're born again, you have no reason to gripe or complain.

If you're lost, you have no reason either because God Almighty has died to save you. If you were the only person alive on the face of the earth, He still would have come and died just for you. That's how much He loves you, and if you remember this, nothing could ever make you gripe and complain.

I believe in the full Gospel—salvation, healing, deliverance, and prosperity. But if God never healed, delivered, or prospered me ever again, the fact that He loves me is enough to keep me shouting and praising His name. If nothing ever worked out for me again in this life, the truth that God redeemed me from hell and I'm heaven bound is more than enough reason to praise Him. He's building a mansion just for me, and I get to spend eternity with Him. No more sorrow, pain, or shame. Hallelujah! I have no reason to gripe or complain. I'm blessed.

Whether you know it or not, you're blessed too. Every believer is blessed. The question is: What have you been valuing? What have you magnified? Where is your attention? Turn your thoughts away from the negative things of this world and put them on the goodness of God. The Lord has been good to you.

Firm in the Face of Contrary

A woman recently told me how someone she had prayed for died. She said, "Without consciously thinking about it, I know this circumstance has devalued my revelation of God. I've been confused and it's hindered my faith."

I've been through that too. I prayed for four people who died before I saw the first one raise from the dead. Although I'd never proposed to her, I was thinking about marrying this girl. We had even talked about it a little bit. Her parents told the Red Cross we were engaged, and I received an emergency leave from Vietnam to come home and see her. I was with her when she died. She drowned to death on her own blood. We prayed over her for more than two hours after she died, but she didn't come back.

That affected me and every other person associated with this. They all said, "It must not be God's will to heal because if anyone was going to be healed, it would have been Debbie." Although I was just as confused and hurt as anyone else, I declared, "God, Your Word says that by Your stripes we were healed." (1 Pet. 2:24.)

The Lord had even given her a special promise:

> I shall not die, but live, and declare the works of the LORD.
>
> PSALM 118:17

I walked out of there saying, "I don't understand it, but this wasn't God's will." And to this day, those people who were associated with that think I've gone off the deep end. Although I had no answers and didn't know what was going on, I maintained this attitude. For three and a half years I had to look at something that was contrary to what God's Word said. But I stood firm saying, "God, Your Word says it and I won't back off. It's true whether I see it or not." I just had to shelve it and go on with God.

"Lord, Your Word Says…"

Three and a half years later, the Lord showed me why it happened. Once I received the revelation, I went over to my neighbor's house. She had the exact same thing Debbie died from—leukemia. I prayed for her and she was healed. Praise God! And to this day, I've seen that truth set many, many people free.

I've been through things, but I've done what I'm sharing with you. Even through gritted teeth at times, I just kept saying, "Lord, Your Word says…" and because of it, I'm still happy in Jesus, walking in victory, and seeing people healed today.

Regardless of what your problems, pressures, and pains are, you can believe God. It's just as simple as glorifying Him. Place value and worth on what He's said and done. Magnify Him, be thankful, and remember His goodness. That's how you stay full of God.

CHAPTER 10

The Power of Imagination

God doesn't cause His joy, peace, anointing, and healing to come and go. (Rom. 11:29.) We do. God isn't the variable. We are. He's not the One who moves in "waves." It's the body of Christ who receives in waves what Jesus has already provided. The Lord is constant, but we're not. He doesn't do "this" for a while, and then change His mind and do "that" instead. Everything Jesus Christ lived, died, and resurrected to provide for us has been constantly available since He sat down at the right hand of the Father.

Just like a television station constantly transmits its signal, God is always transmitting. However, whether we perceive that signal or not depends on our receiver. Is it plugged in, turned on, and tuned in? Whether we experience God's provision or not depends on whether or not we're receiving. If we aren't, the problem is with our receiver, not God's transmitter, and there are specific things we can do to fix our receiver.

The vast majority of the body of Christ begs God for things He's already given. If you pray that way, you're just going to get silence on the other end because God can't do anything that He hasn't already done for you. You just need to learn how to receive what He has already provided.

But after you receive, you must also maintain it. In some ways, it's more important to know how to maintain what you've received than it is to receive God's touch in the first place.

In order to maintain consistency and keep the things of God fresh and alive in your heart, the first key is you must glorify God. This means you must value and prize Him. Many of our problems come as a result of misplaced values. We let other things compete with and occupy the place that God alone should have in our life.

Your Spiritual Smell

The second key is to be thankful. God's Word reveals that we give off a spiritual smell. That's what the word *savour*[1] means in these verses:

> "For we are unto God a sweet savour of Christ, in them that are saved, and in them that perish: To the one we are the savour of death unto death; and to the other the savour of life unto life."
>
> 2 CORINTHIANS 2:15,16

The praise and thanksgiving of the redeemed—like sacrifices in the Old Testament—produces a spiritual aroma that blesses God. However, just like the smell of manure attracts flies, griping and complaining attract demons. Have you wondered why bad things always seem to happen to you? It may be because you're a griper and a complainer. If that's true, you're drawing all of the demons in the county to yourself. You need to be a God-praiser.

Praise is one of the most important things you can do. It makes you focus on what the Lord is doing. If you're the kind of person who tends toward the negative, you won't continue in praising God. If you make a decision to start praising the Lord, you'll have to start seeing the positive side of things. Why? There's nothing praiseworthy in the negative. This forces you to focus on the things of God. (Phil. 4:4-8.)

Counterfeits and Abuse

The third key comes from Romans 1:21 where it says they "became vain in their imaginations."

If you're a leaky vessel, one of the main holes where God leaks out of you is your not glorifying God. That leads to not being thankful. These two things combined cause your imagination to become "vain."

To be *vain* is to be idle or non-productive. It's not that your imagination isn't functioning. It's just not benefiting you.

Many Christians don't like to talk about imagination. They often think it's childish, saying, "Only kids daydream and imagine things. I'm logical and deal only in reality." They pride themselves on being a "realist" instead of a visionary—imaginative—person. Others see imagination as something associated with Eastern religions. "Sit down in a lotus position and visualize world peace." Just because something is abused doesn't mean we should chuck it.

Eastern religions abuse prayer too, but that doesn't mean you should quit praying. Satan only counterfeits something that's real. The very fact that other people have counterfeited this shows that it has genuine value.

It's Always Working

Your imagination is important. It's functioning all the time. You may think, *I'm not a person who sits around imagining things,* but you are—constantly. It's how you do everything. You don't have a choice whether your imagination works or not. You just get to choose whether it's working for or against you.

If you quit glorifying, magnifying, praising, and thanking God, your imagination will automatically gravitate toward negative things. You can't control that. Your imagination is basically a by-product of your focus. If you are really valuing the things of God—praising and thanking Him—your imagination will begin to see things happening properly in your life.

Whether you realize it or not, your mind functions through imagination. You can't really do anything about it. As a matter of fact, the word *imaginations* in the Old Testament literally means "a form"[2] and figuratively means "conception."[3] Your imagination is the part of you where you conceive things.

If you didn't have an imagination, you would be totally noncreative. Just like an animal, you'd have to be taught and learn things by repetition. But one of the distinguishing characteristics between human beings and animals is our imagination. It's a powerful part of who we are.

Whether you recognize it or not, your imagination is the part of you that conceives everything. Before you can act anything out, you have to conceive it first in your imagination. If you can't see it with your imagination, you can't do it.

You Think in Pictures

This is why a builder uses blueprints. It's also why, "A picture is worth a thousand words." Your imagination is the part of you that makes things work in your life. It's your ability to see something with your inner eyes instead of your physical eyes. Human beings think in pictures.

If I whispered the word "dog" in your ear right now, you wouldn't just see the letters D-O-G. You'd see a picture of a dog. It would probably be one that you've had or have personally interacted with before. You're not looking at an animal right now, you're looking at a book, but in your mind, you have a picture of a dog.

With my words, I can change your picture. You might be thinking of a poodle or a Chihuahua, but now I'm going to say, "Big dog." Instantly, your picture changes. "Big, black dog," and your image changes again. "Big, black, mean dog," and it'll change again. "Big, black, mean dog with vicious teeth." Do you get the picture? Even though I can use words to influence the image you see, you think in pictures.

What did the house that you grew up in look like? Now, you might have moved several times and several different houses come to mind. But if you lived primarily in one place, the picture of that house will come to mind. If I asked you, "How many bathrooms were there? How many bedrooms?" you'd look at the picture in your mind and count them. You don't have that information stored as facts, but as pictures. That's your imagination.

You can't do anything without your imagination. If I asked you, "How do I get to the airport?" you'd say, "Take a right on the main road out here and go down to the second stoplight. Turn left and get on the highway. Get off on the third exit and follow the signs to the airport. It'll be a mile down on your right." How would you do that? You didn't have that information just stored. You pictured it with your imagination, and then described what you saw to me. But if you'd never been to the airport before, you couldn't have told me where to go. Why? You wouldn't have been able to picture it. That's how you use your imagination.

Negative Use

You use your imagination constantly. It's the conception part of you. You can't build anything without it. Dressmakers depend on a pattern. It helps them picture the dress they're making. Manufacturers give you pictures in the instructions for how to assemble something. There are words of explanation too, but it's the picture of how this part goes together with that part and completes the final product that helps you imagine it.

Your imagination is the creative part of you. This is why it literally means "conception." There can be no creativity without using your imagination. But if you quit glorifying God and being thankful, your imagination is forced to work against you instead of for you. You'll start conceiving and seeing negative things. You'll start being fearful and operating in unbelief instead of faith. This is the negative use of imagination.

The doctor will say, "You have cancer and you're going to die" and instantly your imagination causes you to see yourself in a casket. If you knew someone who suffered and died of cancer, you'll see yourself in that position. Your imagination would just go that way. The sad fact is that most people's imagination is very negative. It's working against you by conceiving all this doubt, fear, unbelief, worry, and hatred.

Void of Speculative Imagination

One of the New Testament qualifications of an elder is to be "sober" (1 Tim. 3:2; Titus 1:8). It's also required of a deacon's wife. (1 Tim. 3:11.) This isn't talking about not being drunk. *Sober* literally means to be void of speculative imagination.

The Lord has really used this in my life. When you first get started in the ministry, you want people to like you. You don't want to go in and cause problems everywhere you speak. You want to be a blessing. However, if you're not careful, you could fall into the trap of ministering for people's acceptance instead of for the Lord.

There was a particular couple that would always drive to my meetings anytime I ministered within a hundred miles of Kansas City. They were just so blessed by my ministry and had become good friends of mine. They never missed a meeting.

Then one time I went to Kansas City and they were noticeably absent. I remembered when I was there the year before how I had given them a very specific prophecy. It wasn't one of those generic prophecies that could apply to anyone. It was very precise. I'd either heard from God 100 percent or totally missed it. There was no compromise.

When I didn't see them, I started thinking, speculating, and imagining. I thought, *I bet I missed it last year and now they're upset with me.* I saw them spreading rumors that I was a false prophet. The more I thought about it, the angrier I became. I was honestly to the point of punching them in the nose!

But the next night they showed up and came over to me saying, "We're so sorry we missed yesterday. We just had a death in the family and couldn't get away. We never would have missed your meeting otherwise." The Lord showed me that I was ready to take up an offense over something that didn't happen. I was speculating—imagining—what they were thinking and what was going on.

"Judge Not"

I've been to so many churches where someone was offended and ready to quit the church just because the pastor didn't speak to them. They imagined that it was because he didn't like them, but they never considered the fact that maybe he had somebody or something else on his mind when he passed by them in the hall. There could have been a million reasons why he didn't greet them. This is what the Bible means when it says:

> "Judge not, that ye be not judged. For with what judgment ye judge, ye shall be judged: and with what measure ye mete, it shall be measured to you again. And why beholdest thou the mote that is in thy brother's eye, but considerest not the beam that is in thine own eye? Or how wilt thou say to thy brother, Let me pull out the mote out of thine eye; and, behold, a beam is in thine own eye? Thou hypocrite, first cast out the beam out of thine own eye; and then shalt thou see clearly to cast out the mote out of thy brother's eye."
>
> MATTHEW 7:1-5

Some people become confused over this because other scriptures tell us to judge. This passage simply says, "With the judgment you judge others with, so you also will be judged. So be merciful. Take the beam out of your own eye first, before you try to take the speck out of someone else's." That's the kind of judgment this passage is referring to.

However, if you found yourself in a big-city alley at night with a man dressed up like a gangster quickly coming toward you with a whip in one hand and a knife in the other—you'd better judge. There's nothing wrong with saying, "This doesn't look good. I'd better get out of here!" It's beneficial to judge this way, but it's wrong to try to figure out why he's dressed that way and doing what he's doing.

This is especially important in relationships. When someone says something that offends you, there's nothing wrong with going up to them and saying, "When you said such and such, it made me feel this way." Wrong judging would be telling them, "What you said is wrong because..." and then you speculate why they said what they did. You don't know why they said it. They may not have realized what they were saying. They probably had no idea that they were offending you. They may have said it because someone else offended them. You don't know why people do what they do.

Why Is Not Your Business

After the Lord showed me this about being sober, I made a decision not to speculate about what's going on. I've even taught my staff this, saying, "I will not accept hints. If you're mad at me or dislike me, you're going to have to come and tell me directly." I can tell when someone isn't acting very friendly, but I refuse to speculate about why. That's their business. If they have something against me, they're going to have to tell me about it themselves. I am not going to speculate about it.

Maybe there's someone you have judged. Perhaps you've already condemned them about why they're doing what they're doing, but you don't honestly know. You don't have a clue as to why they did what they did because you've never asked them. That's speculative imagination.

CHAPTER 11

Inner Images

Your imagination is a powerful force. As a matter of fact, you cannot consistently function contrary to the image you have on the inside.

For as he thinketh in his heart, so *is* he.

PROVERBS 23:7

In your heart, you have an image—a picture—of who you are and what you're like. Sadly, most people haven't let the Word of God paint that picture. Other people and experiences have shaped that image. However, we need to get a picture on the inside of us of who we are in Christ and who He is in us. We need to take God's Word like a paintbrush and change that inner image to agree with what the Word says about us. But most people are living life with a different image.

You may be someone who gives every time the bucket comes by, but you may still see yourself as poor in your heart.

You may fulfill God's Word by sowing and planting lots of seed, but your image of yourself in your heart is one of poverty. You see yourself in lack, and so you are. Your imagination has locked you into this self-fulfilling prophecy. Therefore, you continue to fulfill this image that you have on the inside.

Perhaps you see yourself as an introvert. You're shy and bashful around people. This image will dominate and control you until you change it. I used to be an introvert to the max. I couldn't even look someone in the face and talk to them. But through God's Word, I've totally changed the image on the inside. Now I'm an extrovert to the max. You can change who you are.

A Prosperous Attitude

When we lived in Seagoville, Texas, we were so poor we couldn't even pay attention. We couldn't just go out and buy things. So I started praying over things and believing God. Even though I knew nothing about cars, I began working on them. By faith, I declared, "I can do all things through Christ who strengthens me." (Phil. 4:13.) I repaired cars of problems of which I had no knowledge. I couldn't tell you why they worked, but they did.

Someone gave us a washing machine with a broken brake. I took that thing apart and looked at it, but couldn't figure it out. So I prayed over it and did something to it—and that thing worked for years after that. I just developed an attitude that I can prosper and do anything.

I took a job developing pictures for this guy. I told him, "You'll be blessed because you hired me." His business was on the rocks, but I had this image on the inside of me. Even though I'd never developed pictures before in my life, I figured it out so well that I pulled this fellow's business out of bankruptcy within two months. I turned his business around so much that he offered me an equal partnership—no money up front—if I would just run it for him. He was going to give me 50 percent of the business! However, that's when the Lord called me to Pritchett, Colorado. So I declined his offer and left.

Through all this, I'd been changing my inner image of myself to agree with God's Word. It was my imagination I was dealing with.

Releasing the Word's Power

If you glorify and thank God, your imagination will start conceiving things differently. If you are grateful and place value on what the Lord has said and done in your life, you'll have faith for your future. Instead of being fearful and seeing negative things come to pass, you'll be hopeful and start seeing positive things come to pass.

> Thou wilt keep *him* in perfect peace, *whose* mind *is* stayed on *thee:* because he trusteth in thee.
>
> ISAIAH 26:3

The Hebrew word rendered "mind" here is the exact same word translated "imaginations" in other parts of the Old Testament.[1] So you could say that when your imagination is stayed on the Lord, He'll keep you in perfect peace.

Your imagination is your ability to picture something on the inside. Most people don't use their imagination when it comes to relating to the Lord, but they should.

I use my imagination when I meditate on the Word. The vast majority of the revelation I receive from God doesn't come from just reading the Bible. Now, reading the Word is important because you can't meditate on what you haven't read. Reading the Bible is entering the data into your computer. Without this data entry, there wouldn't be anything for your computer to process. However, after I've read the Word, I sit down and meditate on it. I take the raw data and begin to process it. This is where the real revelation and power is released in Scripture.

Scripture Comes Alive

When I read about David and Goliath (1 Sam. 17), I wanted to picture how tall this giant was. Since our ceilings were only eight feet high, I had to go outside the house to make this mark. Then I stood next to this nine and a half foot mark and pictured what it was really like to go up against this giant.

Why is going to the Holy Land such a life-changing experience? Why does it make the Word come alive so much? It's not that the presence of the Lord is so much greater in Israel than anywhere else in the world today. It's just that being there enables your imagination to see things in the Word more clearly.

I remember going down to the Valley of Elah. I left the bus and walked down to the little stream there. Then I picked up five smooth stones—exactly the way David did—to help me picture what was going on. When you can picture what the Word of God is talking about, it just comes alive.

After you've read the information—data entry—sit down and let the Holy Spirit guide your imagination. Don't just let your mind think about anything. If you've been putting junk into your imagination from television or whatever, it may head in the wrong direction. But if you allow the Word of God to control your thoughts and start thinking about the scriptures you just read, you'll start seeing things in the Word—processing the data—that you can't see with your physical eyes. You must see it on the inside with your imagination.

When the Bible says that you're healed, you must take this and meditate on it until you see yourself healed. Most people see themselves sick, not healed. They see the pain and hurt. They already have a clear picture of themselves deteriorating. They've been told what's going to happen, and what each stage will be like. They're constantly checking themselves to see where they are in this progression. They see the end result of death, pain, or whatever. You need to say, "That's not what I see in the Word!" Then take scriptures and meditate on them until your imagination sees yourself running, jumping, sleeping through the night, living without pain, or whatever it is that you're overcoming.

Greater Works

This is how I first saw people raised from the dead. I took the Word of God and meditated on it.

Verily, verily, I say unto you, He that believeth on me, the works that I do shall he do also; and greater *works* than these shall he do; because I go unto my Father.

JOHN 14:12

I started speaking it and talking about it. I took all of the scriptures where people were raised from the dead—nine if you include Jesus—and meditated on them. I'd close my eyes and imagine myself there saying, "Lazarus, come forth!" and he did. (See John 11:43–44.) I saw myself doing all those things Jesus did. I thought about it so much that I started having dreams about raising people from the dead. Then I started actually seeing people raised from the dead.

There's a reason this happens for some people and not for others. If you can't see it on the inside, you won't see it on the outside. Why? Your imagination is where the conception takes place. Most people are just letting the physical input of their eyes control their imagination. But the Word of God will paint a picture that can replace those natural things.

Maybe you've never seen someone with a broken arm instantly healed. But if you meditate on it until you start seeing it on the inside, then you can see it happen on the outside. Perhaps you've never seen anyone in the situation you're in set free, but you can find it in God's Word. If you'll meditate on it, you can conceive it, begin seeing it, and it will change things.

Evil Imaginations

Although Genesis 6 records the negative use of imagination, it's still a powerful example.

> And GOD saw that the wickedness of man was great in the earth, and *that* every imagination of the thoughts of his heart *was* only evil continually.
>
> GENESIS 6:5

Even though many of us have had an encounter with the Lord, been born again and baptized in the Holy Spirit, the truth is that the vast majority of our imaginations are evil. We see negative things—things contrary to God's Word. We see ourselves failing, angry, bitter, and rejected. We see ourselves in ways that are contrary to what God's Word says, and most of us just allow our imagination to run rampant. We don't honestly think that there is anything wrong with imagining things, but this verse shows us that God saw the imagination of the thoughts of their heart.

David gave instructions to his son right before he died and Solomon became king. He said:

> And thou, Solomon my son, know thou the God of thy father, and serve him with a perfect heart and with a willing mind: for the LORD searcheth all hearts, and understandeth all the imaginations of the thoughts: if thou seek him, he will

be found of thee; but if thou forsake him, he will cast thee off for ever.

1 CHRONICLES 28:9

God sees all the imaginations of the heart. If you look through the rest of the Old Testament, you'll find at least half a dozen times where the Lord brought judgment on people for their imaginations.

Spiritual Conception

Most of us focus on our actions. We think, *I can't go out and commit adultery. I can't do it!* But it's stupid to allow your imagination to think on and conceive that, and then have to fight, resist, and try to keep from acting out what you've thought on in your heart.

That's like a woman who doesn't want to birth a child, but isn't placing any restrictions whatsoever upon having physical relationships. She's constantly conceiving, but then having to abort in order to keep from having a birth. This isn't the way not to have children. If you don't want to conceive, don't have a physical relationship.

In the spiritual realm, most of us don't recognize that our imagination is where we conceive. There are very few things you can watch on television that won't give you negative imaginations. Programs are constantly presenting sexual situations. Most shows will teach you how to get angry, bitter, and fight back, but the Word says to forgive and turn the other cheek. (Luke 6:29.) Whether you realize it or not, those visual images are painting pictures on the inside of you. When you come into a crisis or some other similar temptation, you'll be tempted to act that out because it's already been conceived.

You can literally reach a place where you don't conceive things—and if you can't conceive it, you can't do it. You can actually get to a place where you don't know how to sin. "Come on, Andrew. You can't be serious." I am—and you can do it. You can literally get your mind so stayed on God that all it's doing is conceiving joy, peace, and power. If you keep your imagination stayed on Him, you'll be in perfect peace. (Isa. 26:3.)

Rampant Thoughts

We cause ourselves a tremendous amount of problems because of the way we allow our imaginations to think. Very few people feel any responsibility for their imagination. Very few even know what their imagination is. They just allow their thoughts to run rampant and they think on negative things.

Someone came to me once and asked, "Do you think I married the wrong person? I'm having trouble in my marriage. Do you think I missed God?" They honestly wanted me to help them decide whether they had missed God or not. I told them, "That's stupid. It doesn't matter whether you've made a mistake or not. Never—never think that stuff. There is absolutely nothing positive that could ever come of it, but there's a tremendous amount of damage that could. What are you going to do? Divorce your spouse? Go get another one and violate the Scripture? That is not an option. You should never let your thoughts go there."

There are things that come against me that I refuse to think. I could sit down and imagine all kinds of bad things. When we first started out on television, it significantly increased our expenses. I had to consider some of these things to see how much money we needed so I could make some plans and communicate with our partners. I thought on some of these things, but I've never allowed myself one time to see myself fail in this endeavor. I've never allowed my mind to go there and imagine what I'd have to do if we didn't have the money and I had to back up, go off, and say, "I missed it." I've never thought it or gone there in my mind because that's not what God told me.

I refuse to think things contrary to what God's Word says. Therefore, I don't conceive it and I'm not tempted with it.

When God tells most people something to do, they immediately sit down and figure out every reason why it won't work. They allow their imagination to go down that road and see themselves failing. Then, after they've considered all of this junk, they say, "God, can I believe You for this?" That's like trying to swim with weights on. It's not going to work, and it's not the way God wants you to do it.

Don't Go There

Most of us don't understand how important our imagination is. Maybe every once in awhile, you get depressed and say, "I'd feel better if I just got down and had a pity party." So you sit down and start thinking, *Nobody loves me. Everyone hates me.* But you know it's not true.

When you do that, you're acting just like Elijah. "God, I'm the only one left!" (1 Kings 19:10). Yet Obadiah had told him that there were still a hundred preachers left that he had hidden in a cave and fed with bread and water. (1 Kings 18:3-4,7,13.) Although Elijah knew better, he started to whine, "Oh God, I'm the only one left." He allowed himself to get into a pity party and left this life after obeying only one of the three final instructions God gave him in 1 Kings 19:15-16, which was to anoint his replacement.

"But Andrew, I just feel better when I get down, gripe, complain, and throw myself a pity party." Don't go there! Don't allow your thoughts to go there. Don't see yourself failing. Don't see your prayers not being answered. You may say, "Surely, I can't live this way." I say, "Yes, you can."

Some people are so negative that all it takes is the devil to whisper a word and they make a paragraph out of it. He can just go on vacation because they're so wonderful at amplifying and magnifying the negative. They have a little pain in their chest and think it's a heart attack. Then they meditate on it until they actually are having a heart attack because of the fear. But the truth was, it was nothing to start with. People take the smallest thing and amplify it.

Your imagination does that. Most people's imagination is evil. They go in the wrong direction.

CHAPTER 12

Prepare Your Heart

David gave an offering of $1.5 billion worth of gold and silver from his personal bank account. (1 Chron. 29.) Although he'd already given $5 billion toward the building of the temple from his government treasuries, this gift was from his own personal wealth. Not bad for a shepherd boy!

David was prosperous. When he gave, the people were so blessed that they started giving spontaneously too—to the amount of $3.5 billion. So altogether, it was a $5 billion spontaneous offering!

> Then the people rejoiced, for that they offered willingly, because with perfect heart they offered willingly to the LORD: and David the king also rejoiced with great joy.
>
> 1 CHRONICLES 29:9

Then David started praying in verse 10. He glorified God—recognized and acknowledged Him. What had happened that day was supernatural and he placed value on it, thanking God and saying, "Lord, all we've done is give You that which was already Yours. Everything we have, You gave it to us in the first place." (vv. 14–17.) David started thanking God for the blessing, remembering where it came from, glorifying and thanking Him. Then in verse 18, he said:

> O LORD God of Abraham, Isaac, and of Israel, our fathers, *keep this for ever in the imagination of the thoughts of the heart of thy people,* and prepare their heart unto thee.
>
> 1 CHRONICLES 29:18

David was saying, "Lord, help us remember!"

Make Monuments

Memory is powerful. Your imagination is the part of you that remembers. My teaching entitled "How to Prepare Your Heart" will tell you much more about it than I can here.

But 2 Chronicles 12:14 says:

> [Rehoboam] did evil, because he prepared not his heart to seek the LORD.

Preparing your heart is vital—and remembering is one of the most important things you can do to prepare your heart.

I've prepared my heart to seek the Lord. Even though it's been almost four decades since God supernaturally intervened in my life, I've been glorifying God, thanking Him, and remembering what He's said and done.

I make monuments in my life constantly. We just drove through Arlington, Texas, so we took some time and saw our old house. I drove by the field where I received the baptism in the Holy Spirit. I also have that boulder that rolled over my hand, arm, and head where we live now to remind me of God's goodness. I'm not going to forget that Jesus saved my life because I walk by it almost every day. Memory makes a huge difference.

"Whose Fault Is It?"

After getting married, most people start dealing with all the pressures of daily life and forget those things that really made them fall in love with their mate in the first place. They forget the good things, and start focusing on the negative. Then their imagination begins to magnify them. Do you know what? You can't live with someone if you don't remember anything good about them.

I've actually sat down with married couples before and said, "There's something good in that person. Tell me something good about them."

And they've answered, "I can't think of anything good in my mate."

So I ask them, "Did you love them when you got married?" "Oh yeah, they were great!"

"Well then, if they were okay when you got them, guess whose fault it is that they turned out this way?"

Your memory is a very important force!

"God Saved My Life!"

> He that lacketh these things is blind, and cannot see afar off, and hath forgotten that he was purged from his old sins.
>
> 2 PETER 1:9

You can actually forget what Jesus has done for you. I've had people come up to me who were so upset they were going to walk away from God. But I just started reminding them of what He had done. Then everything changed once they remembered.

A few years ago in Chicago, I called out through the gifts of the Holy Spirit that someone had tried to commit suicide or was thinking about it. When this woman came forward, she started telling me how everything in her life had gone wrong. As I prayed for her, the Holy Spirit gave me four instances where Satan had tried to kill her from the time she was a little girl. So I reminded her of them, saying, "Do you remember when you were four years old and someone tried to rape and kill you? You focused on the negative side, but look what happened. The Lord says that they tried to kill you and it was a miracle you lived. Instead of magnifying the negative, you ought to say, 'God saved my life!'" Then I went through the other three things He showed me and reminded her of them. By the time she got through remembering how the Lord had delivered her, this woman—who had been contemplating suicide—was on her knees praising and thanking God for His grace and mercy.

God has done some awesome things for each and every one of us. There's no reason why you should be upset, except that you forget the goodness of God. Your memory is a vital part of your life. Your imagination is how you remember things. You must start using your imagination in a positive way.

How Great Thou Art

Wherefore I will not be negligent to put you always in remembrance of these things.

2 PETER 1:12

Your memory needs to be stirred up. You need to remember things over and over and over again.

Moreover I will endeavour that ye may be able after my decease to have these things always in remembrance.

2 PETER 1:15

This second epistle, beloved, I now write unto you; in *both* which I stir up your pure minds by way of remembrance.

2 PETER 3:1

You can stir yourself up through memory. Almost ten years ago I was in a service in Lima, Ohio. There were 600 people and we had seen so many good things happen during our time together. There were actually people standing outside the building and listening through the open windows. We started singing "How Great Thou Art" and I had a flashback to my father's funeral. That had been my dad's favorite song. I remembered sitting there as a twelve-year-old boy thinking, *God, this doesn't compute. My dad just died and we're singing about how great You are.* I remembered praying, "If You really are great, reveal Yourself to me and give me a purpose for my life." I was overwhelmed with God's faithfulness as that memory brought me to my knees. A memory can stir you powerfully.

Disconnected

Yet, very few of us take time to remember. It takes effort to remember. You have to be still, turn off the television, shut off the radio, and spend time reflecting. You ought to spend some quiet time each and every day just remembering. If you did, you'd find out it would transform your life. It's your imagination that does this. Go back and picture things.

My mother and I were over in Marietta, Texas, a short time ago talking to people who knew our relatives, and remembering things. Every time I get a chance, I go to these places that have been really significant in my life. I just sit there and remember. Those are some of the most powerful times I have, and it really makes a difference in my life.

Our whole society is getting away from this. Do you know much about your grandparents? What about your great-grandparents? As a whole, we are a society that lives life so into the moment and occupied with our own self that we don't know these things.

While in England recently, I preached in a pastor friend's church. Then he took us to his home for lunch afterwards. His family had lived in the exact same house since the 1400s. He took me into the house and said, "Right here is where my great, great, great, great, great-grandfather was born, and here is where they were married." He knew this. As he was sharing this information, I was thinking, *Man, the history this guy lives with! How would that impact his life and his actions? How would knowing what his grandparents had done in this house and how they conducted themselves enter into his reasoning and the things he does today?* Most of us are so disconnected from anything like that. We don't even like to think about it.

Memory is a powerful force. That's the reason the Lord told us to erect monuments and not tear down our neighbor's landmark.(Gen. 35:1; Deut. 19:14.)

"Don't You Remember?"

You need to rehearse your victories. When the Lord rebuked David for his sin with Bathsheba, He said, "David, don't you remember that I took you from following the sheep? Don't you remember that your name wasn't even put in the hat when Samuel came? You were out keeping the sheep. They didn't even esteem you enough to think you had a chance of becoming king. Don't you remember what I did? How I overcame your enemies? Don't you remember how I gave you all of these things? If that wasn't enough, I would have given you more!" (2 Sam. 12:7-8.) God referred him back to memory.

In order for you to go out and do some of the things you do, you have to forget the goodness and faithfulness of God. I'm not encouraging anyone to try this, but what would happen if right before a man jumped into bed with a prostitute, he said, "Let's just pray and dedicate this to the Lord.

Let's just take a moment and thank God for His goodness." I bet it would ruin the whole thing. That's what remembering the goodness of God will do to you—it'll ruin sin in your life.

All four of these keys to staying full of God are interrelated. Glorify God. Be thankful. Remember. If you were doing these things on a consistent basis, it would create an atmosphere of God's goodness and faithfulness in your life. It would prevent you from doing some of the things that you do. Your imagination would start focusing on positive things. Instead of seeing yourself fail, you'd see God's goodness and things working out.

A worrywart is just someone with a vivid imagination in the negative realm. If you're anxious about things, your imagination is functioning in the wrong direction. But the good news is that you can turn that around. You need to start using your imagination in the right way.

CHAPTER 13

What Do You See?

And when the day was now far spent, his disciples came unto him, and said, This is a desert place, and now the time *is* far passed: Send them away, that they may go into the country round about, and into the villages, and buy themselves bread: for they have nothing to eat. He answered and said unto them, Give ye them to eat.

MARK 6:35-37

The disciples saw the need, but they didn't see themselves as having the ability to meet it. They wanted to send the people somewhere else to have their needs met.

The church is doing this today. We're sending people to psychologists, bankers, doctors, and lawyers, when in reality we're the ones who have the answer. They don't have to depart. We could meet their needs, but most of the body of Christ doesn't see that. We don't see ourselves as being able to heal the sick, cleanse the lepers, or raise the dead, so we send them somewhere else. The Lord said, "They don't need to depart. You give them something to eat." Most of us think, *But that's unreasonable!* Jesus wouldn't have asked them—or us—to do something they couldn't have done. They could have fed these people. They had the ability to do it. But they had never seen themselves as able to feed five thousand people before.

> And they say unto him, Shall we go and buy two hundred pennyworth of bread, and give them to eat?
>
> MARK 6:37

They pulled their wallet out of their pocket and peeked inside. They looked at their natural resources instead of their spiritual resources.

Receive Spiritual Sight

> He saith unto them, How many loaves have ye? go and see. And when they knew, they say, Five, and two fishes. And he commanded them to make all sit down by companies upon the green grass. And they sat down in ranks, by hundreds, and by fifties. And when he had taken the five loaves and the two fishes, *he looked up to heaven,* and blessed, and brake the loaves, and gave *them* to his disciples to set before them; and the two fishes divided he among them all.
>
> MARK 6:38-41

When Jesus looked up to heaven, He did more than just lift His head. This Greek word—*anablepo*—is a combination of *blepo* and *ana*. *Blepo* means "to see"[1] and *ana*—when used in a compound like this—means "again."[2] Jesus literally saw twice or saw again.

This same word is translated "receive sight" fifteen times in the Bible. When Bartimaeus received his sight, the word used is *anablepo*.[3] (Mark 10:51.) When others' blind eyes opened, the word used is *anablepo*.[4] (Matt. 20:34.) It's this same word.

So when Jesus looked up, He saw twice. He saw differently than His disciples. Do you know what He did? He saw on the inside. He saw in the spirit realm instead of seeing with His physical eyes. The disciples were looking at their physical resources and so they were limited to what they could see, taste, hear, smell, and feel. Jesus could see past the physical and into the spiritual realm. That's what Mark 6:41 is talking about.

When He looked up, He didn't just lift up His head, He perceived the situation with His spiritual eyes. In other words, it's talking about His imagination. He had a pure mind that was able to see things by faith. He wasn't limited to what He physically saw with His eyes. He could see whatever God's Word said.

Jesus saw with His spiritual eyes that these five loaves and two fish were enough. The disciples looked at them and at the crowd and saw it wasn't enough. Most of us look at the little bit we have and at the need and say, "Oh God, it's not enough. I'll never make it!" We curse what we have. Jesus blessed it instead. We say, "Oh God, I could never do what You've called me to do. I can't preach!" But Jesus blessed.

Then He fed five thousand men—and that's not including the women and children. He fed over ten thousand people with five loaves and two fish, and the fragments left over after everyone's seconds and thirds added up to much more than what they started with.

See by Faith

Think of the logistics. If Jesus had broken the bread and multiplied it all in His hands, and then given it to the disciples to run back and forth distributing to all these groups of people, this would have taken at least seven hours (For a detailed explanation, please see the footnote for Luke 9:16 on page 177 of my *Life for Today: Gospels Edition."* This Bible commentary is also available free online at our Web site). However, it's much more likely that the Lord broke the bread once and gave it to the disciples. Then they went out with one little fish and one piece of bread, which they started breaking, giving, and seeing multiply in their hands.

So Jesus, in effect, blessed this food and gave it to His disciples. Then they had to have a lot of faith to walk toward each group of fifty hungry people with just this little bit of food and start passing it out. Some of them could have stopped and said, "But Jesus, I need more!" They didn't need more. They had enough. That one little loaf and that one little fish were more than enough for thousands of people when they were blessed. But they had to see it spiritually.

Whatever you have is more than enough if you could get your imagination renewed so that you didn't see with your physical eyes. If you saw your true potential, you could start seeing with your heart what God has really given you.

Take God's Word and let it paint a picture on the inside of you. Let it show you that you have the same power that raised Christ from the dead living on the inside of you. (Rom. 8:11.) You don't need to plead with God to give you something more. You just need to look up, receive sight, and see what you already have. If you would do that, you could go to the masses and see people saved, healed, and delivered. You'd have words to say and you could flow in the gifts of the Holy Spirit. Anything you'd need would function.

But the problem is we aren't looking up. We aren't receiving spiritual sight. We aren't seeing with our inner man. We aren't using our imagination to see ourselves like God sees us. We're looking in the mirror instead. We're listening to what everybody else thinks about us. We're looking at other churches and thinking, *Well, do other people do this?* We're making comparisons and letting other people paint the image inside us. You need to go to God's Word and find out what He says about you. That's who you are and that's what you can do. You need to see yourself that way.

How Do You See Yourself?

Most Christians have never seen their real self. If I asked someone what they looked like, they would describe to me their outward man, but they probably wouldn't know who they are in Christ. Due to this, we live like beggars—poor, depressed, and defeated. God has already given us everything, but we just haven't seen it.

Jesus prayed for a blind man and made him—*anablepo*—look up. (Mark 8:25.)[5] He received his sight and his eyes were opened. You need to get the eyes of your heart opened and the way you do this is to glorify God. Start putting value on and magnifying Him. Take Scripture and say, "Jesus, You are above every name. Cancer has a name. Poverty has a name. If I can name this thing, then You're above it!" Make God bigger in your own eyes than this situation. Then start thanking Him for all the things He's already done. Use your memory to rehearse your victories. If you did all that, your imagination would start seeing good things happen instead of bad. You'd start seeing yourself succeed instead of fail. Your imagination would start functioning for you instead of against you. Then your imagination wouldn't be vain. (Rom. 1:21.)

But if you don't glorify God, be thankful, and remember His goodness, then you're going to be a negative person. One little whisper from the devil and your imagination will run wild with it and see him destroying your life. That's where most people are today.

Your imagination is important. You don't get to choose whether or not it functions. You just get to choose which direction it goes—for you or against you.

If your imagination is vain, then your foolish heart will be darkened (v. 21). You cannot function contrary to your heart. Your heart is the most important aspect.

Ignorant, Lazy, or a Doer?

This is so simple that you have to have somebody help you to misunderstand it. I haven't talked about a single hard thing yet. Everything I've shared has been super simple.

But people would rather go to great effort than renew their mind. They'd rather organize a million people to pray for God to pour out His Spirit and move and make them victorious without glorifying God and being thankful. "Just pour out the Holy Spirit so I can go back to my television and watch my soap operas and talk shows. I don't want to have to spend effort focusing my attention on God and using my mind." People try every way they can to circumvent this and put it back on God: "Bring in an evangelist to do it."

If you would consistently glorify God, be thankful, and use your imagination in a positive way, it would be impossible for you to fail. That doesn't mean you won't have problems. They'll come, but you'll succeed. The inner pressure of God in your life would overcome the outward pressure of the world, circumstances, and the devil. It's just that simple.

Ignorance and laziness are the only two reasons why people don't latch on to this. Either they haven't seen it, or they just don't want to put forth any effort toward it. They want somebody else to wave their hand over them and make it happen. Well, you can't claim ignorance anymore. Are you going to be a doer of the Word or not? It really is that simple. This will change your life!

CHAPTER 14

Warfare and the Heart

Some people have trouble mixing grace and faith together. They tend to lean toward one or the other.

Grace-oriented people say, "God does everything by grace, so we have absolutely nothing to do with it." Well, that's not exactly true. God is God, and He does love you independent of your performance. He does have a perfect plan for every single person, and His grace toward you is totally unmerited. There is nothing you can do to make God's grace abound in you any more than what He's already done. But consider what 1 Corinthians 15:10 says:

> But by the grace of God I am what I am: and his grace which *was bestowed* upon me was not in vain; *but I laboured more abundantly than they all: yet not I, but the grace of God which was with me.*

God's grace is toward every one of us. He has a perfect plan for your life. God has already healed every person. He's already provided abundantly. He's commanded a financial blessing on you. There is no need for you to ever have financial problems. God has already blessed you with financial prosperity and given you perfect health. The same power that raised Christ from the dead is on the inside of every born-again believer. You already have love, joy, and peace. There's never a moment in your born-again life that you don't have these things just flooding in your spirit.

But there are things you can do to release what God has done in the spirit realm and make it manifest in the natural. You can either experience the eternal life of God that resides within your born-again spirit or just keep it dammed up in there.

What you do doesn't affect God's heart toward you, but it will affect your heart toward Him. If you aren't seeking God, He'll love you exactly the same, but you won't love Him the same. You'll be hardened in your heart toward God. There is a balance between grace and faith.

My teachings entitled *Living in the Balance of Grace* and *Faith, Spirit, Soul, & Body,* and *You've Already Got It!* all go into much greater detail about these things. I highly recommend them to you.

Unclog Your Pipe

Faith is your positive response to what God has already given you by grace. Many people don't understand this. When they feel empty, depressed, and discouraged, they're asking God to do something. The Lord has already commanded His blessing upon you. You never have to ask Him to bless you, heal you, give you joy, or love you. God has already given all those things to you. If you aren't experiencing them, it's your pipe that's clogged—not God's.

Since God's transmitter is always transmitting, we need to check our receiver to see whether or not we're receiving. We need to work on ourselves, and our receiving. This is what we've been talking about.

Romans 1:21 reveals four progressive things we do to block the flow of God in our life. But if we turn them around and use them positively instead, they become four keys to staying full of God.

The first key to maintaining the flow of God in your life is to glorify Him. This means to value, prize, honor, and esteem God properly. It also means to magnify—make bigger. You can magnify God and make Him bigger in your life. As you focus on the Lord and place value on what He's said and done, He'll become bigger to you than your circumstances and problems. But first you must esteem Him as more valuable than anything else in your life. This is where most people miss it. They don't properly recognize and value what the Lord has done in their life.

The second key is being thankful. We live in a thankless generation. Being unthankful is unholy. (2 Tim. 3:2.) It's a sin. However, most people see being thankful as a by-product of things going good. "If my life were going good, I'd be thankful." The truth is you should be thankful for what you have right now. If you're waiting until everything in your life is perfect before you're thankful, you'll never be thankful.

Captive and Obedient

The third key is understanding the power of your imagination.

> For though we walk in the flesh, we do not war after the flesh: (For the weapons of our warfare *are* not carnal, but mighty through God to the pulling down of strong holds;) Casting down imaginations, and every high thing that exalteth itself against the knowledge of God, and bringing into captivity every thought to the obedience of Christ.
>
> 2 CORINTHIANS 10:3-5

In case you haven't figured it out yet, there is warfare in the Christian life. If you really commit yourself to the Lord once you're born again, it's like you have a great big target painted on you. The devil is definitely going to come against you. Some people reason, "Well then, I don't want to commit myself to the Lord." But I'm not saying you lose. You can win. In fact, I'm more victorious now than I've ever been, but it isn't because I don't have fights. I have more fights now than I've ever had, but I'm winning. I'm not preaching defeat. I'm just saying that there is warfare.

It takes effort to be able to walk in victory. This scripture says that the weapons of our warfare tear down strongholds, imaginations, and high things that exalt themselves against the knowledge of God. These weapons bring all these thoughts into the captivity and obedience of Christ.

A Diversion

Most of what we hear about spiritual warfare floating around the body of Christ today is absolutely wrong. It's a diversionary tactic. One of the things an enemy tries to do in battle is make you think they're attacking in a certain place. Then, as you marshal all your forces over there, they attack your flank. This is what the devil has been doing.

Satan has been encouraging a lot of this spiritual warfare stuff. People are busy binding this and fighting that. They're trying to do "warfare" with demonic powers over cities, countries, and other areas, but that's not where the battle is.

Scripture says the true battle is in your thoughts and imagination. (2 Cor. 10:3-5.) Spiritual warfare is right between your ears!

People try to "bind" the devil out of a service. In the denominational church I grew up in, we used to "plead the blood" over all the doors and windows. We thought that if the devil could get in there through the blood, he'd have to be a saved devil. It doesn't work that way.

Satan was present at the Last Supper. The Word says he immediately entered into Judas. (John 13:26-27.) This means he had to be right there in the room. If Jesus couldn't keep the devil out of the Last Supper, then you can't keep him out of your meetings. If we could bind the devil and keep him out of our meetings, very few people would come.

The Battle and the Link

It's not what's going on externally that's the issue. The battle is internal—right between your ears. You're fighting thoughts and imaginations. Can you see how important your imagination is?

Most people don't recognize the positive side of imagination—dreams, hopes, goals, and aspirations. But they do recognize the negative side—fear, worry, and dread. How you see things on the inside is actually a driving force in your life.

Your imagination is where you conceive things. If your imagination isn't working for you, then it's working against you—making you creatively sterile. If it's working against you, all you'll be able to do is bring negative things to pass. This is super-important.

Romans 1:21 reveals the link between glorifying God, being thankful, and your imagination working properly. They're all interrelated and connected. You can't just work on your imagination without glorifying God and being thankful. It's the opposite. If you esteem God above everyone and everything else and really begin to praise Him, your imagination will automatically move toward the positive. If you'll place the proper value on the Lord and begin expressing your gratefulness to Him for all He's said and done, your imagination will start functioning in a positive way. You need to understand this.

But if you don't glorify God, aren't thankful, and your imagination becomes vain, then the last step is your foolish heart becomes darkened. (Rom. 1:21.)

Tearing Yourself Apart?

Your heart is a major topic in the Bible. There is a huge amount of material in the Word to help you understand your heart. My teachings *Hardness of Heart* and *How to Prepare*

Your Heart only begin to scratch the surface of what God's Word reveals.

Jesus said:

> Out of the abundance of the heart the mouth speaketh.
> MATTHEW 12:34

Your heart controls what you say and do. It's the essence of who you are.

> As he thinketh in his heart, so *is* he.
> PROVERBS 23:7

Most people don't understand this. They're into what's called "behavior modification." They are trying to change their actions without changing their heart.

People don't realize that their value system is what caused them to act that way in the first place. They get drunk or high on dope. They have a car wreck and lose their job. Finally, they realize that their actions are destroying their life and endangering other people. It's causing problems and putting them in big trouble.

So they try to change their actions without changing their heart. What are they actually doing? They're tearing themselves apart. God's Word calls this "hypocrisy."

Hypocrisy

The body of Christ—to a large degree—puts all of the emphasis on actions. They preach, "Don't dip or cuss or chew—or go with those that do! Praise God, you have to do this, and this, and this, and not do that, and that, and that." The emphasis is placed on actions, but not on changing the heart. Therefore, it's actually creating hypocrisy in people.

The reason many Christians give isn't because they understand giving properly and have a giving heart. They do so out of a fear of punishment. They give—act—but not with the right motive and attitude. Due to this, they aren't able to receive the full benefit of their actions.

> Though I bestow all my goods to feed *the poor*, and though I give my body to be burned, and have not charity [God's kind of love], it profiteth me nothing.
>
> 1 CORINTHIANS 13:3

It doesn't matter what you do, God's Word plainly reveals that your heart attitude is more important than your action. (For more about how this applies to your giving, please refer to my teachings entitled *Financial Stewardship, The Grace of Giving,* and *Grace and Faith in Giving.*)

Jesus told the Pharisees:

Woe unto you, scribes and Pharisees, hypocrites! for ye make clean the outside of the cup and of the platter, but within they are full of extortion and excess. *Thou* blind Pharisee, *cleanse first that which is within the cup and platter, that the outside of them may be clean also.* Woe unto you, scribes and Pharisees, hypocrites! for ye are like unto whited sepulchres, which indeed appear beautiful outward, but are within full of dead *men's* bones, and of all uncleanness.

MATTHEW 23:25-27

The Lord is more concerned about your heart than your actions. If your heart is right, then your actions will be too.

God Is After Your Heart

This sounds good on the surface, but religious people hate to apply it. They're more into the form and outward action than truly dealing with the heart. Some folks are all hung up about external things. If someone came to your church with a heart to know God, but violated your dress code, would you judge them? If they clapped when they shouldn't clap, and shouted praises out loud in your quiet church, would you judge them?

Man looketh on the outward appearance, but the LORD looketh on the heart.

1 SAMUEL 16:7

If you give your heart to God, your actions will eventually change. There's an important relationship here, but people tend to look only on the outward appearance.

Most of religion is human operated. It's according to man's ideas, so they put all of the emphasis on outward appearance. They don't care if your heart is in it or not, as long as they see you cleaned up, and looking and acting like them. Just come to church dressed the right way, do the right things, and put your money in the plate because it doesn't matter to them what your heart is like.

But it does matter to God. He's into changing your heart. Even in your own individual life, it's amazing how much emphasis you put on your actions and ignore the status of your heart. You need to realize that God is after your heart. That's what pleases Him.

CHAPTER 15

Live from Your Heart

While ministering in Phoenix, I noticed this gal who was literally bouncing up and down on the front row. She was excited because she had just been born again two months before. So one night I asked her to come up and share her testimony.

She stood up and said, "Oh, this is the best blankety-blank…" and every third word was profanity. People gasped and some laughed. She looked at me and asked, "Did I do something wrong?"

I answered, "No, you didn't do anything wrong. Just keep going."

So she continued sharing her testimony and cussing up a storm for ten minutes. After the service, people came up to me and said, "I can't believe you let her say that in church. I would never do that!" They criticized her vocabulary—judging her outward man and totally missing her heart.

I told them, "Do you know what? God was more pleased with that testimony than He's been with yours in the last twenty years. Some of you are straight as a gun barrel and twice as empty. You have the mannerisms and behaviors, but your heart isn't on fire for God. You'd never cuss except when you smash your thumb or something goes wrong. You've just learned how to control yourself in church. This woman loves God with all her heart. Her brain just hasn't caught up yet."

When I returned a year later, she came up to me and apologized saying, "I'm sorry! I didn't know Christians don't talk like that. I'd been out in the world. I was a prostitute and thought everybody talked like that. I didn't know I was doing anything wrong." I just gave her some time, and it worked out.

"She'll Learn"

We led a certain lady to the Lord in Childress, Texas. She and her husband had lived in a nudist colony for the three years before. Although this woman was born again, all she had when she first came to church was short shorts. I mean, she could hardly sit on them they were so short! She also had a halter top—and this was a well-endowed lady. We used to sit in a semicircle in this little church. Since we only had about fifty people max, it was impossible not to get in front of her at times. When we started dancing and praising God, it just left nothing to your imagination!

Anyway, the religious people in this church came up to me criticizing and demanding, "Aren't you going to do something about this?"

I responded, "Did we have to throw a sheet over her in the park before we witnessed to her and told her how much Jesus loved her? Give her time, she'll learn." I think it took her about six weeks, but it wasn't very long.

One day she was in a women's Bible study that my wife was leading. She said, "You know, I've never owned a dress in my life. I'd really like to have one and start dressing like the rest of you. Would you all pray that we would get enough money to buy a dress?" By two o'clock that afternoon, she had a dozen dresses! They were all up to the neck and all the way down to the floor. She came to the next church service wearing her dress so proud. Never once did anyone have to tell her, "God is upset and doesn't love you if you don't dress a certain way."

I believe that you should dress in a way that keeps other people from lusting after you. You shouldn't encourage it. But that's something that comes with growth. God looks at your heart. This woman was seeking Him with all her heart. I believe the Lord would have been displeased if we had come up to her, taken her attention off of Him, and put it on all these externals. In my heart, I knew the Lord would show her these things, and He did.

Actions Are By-products

Most religious people just can't handle that. They are so focused on getting others to act right that it causes hypocrisy. They put the emphasis on conforming to this standard whether the individual really wants to or not. So they give in to be accepted or whatever. This breeds hypocrisy. We just catch the fish. It's the Lord's job to clean them. Be tolerant and loving—and let God work on their heart.

The condition of your heart dictates how you act. Some people try to change their actions without changing their heart. That's not the way it's supposed to be. God wants to change your heart, and then your actions will change as a by-product. Actions aren't the driving force—they follow. Right actions are a by-product of an intimate relationship with God.

I'm not telling you not to act godly. I'm just saying that it needs to come from your heart or it doesn't please God. It may please your religion and score points with certain people, but God looks on your heart.

It doesn't matter that you're doing the right things. You could give all you have to feed the poor, and even die a martyr's death, but if you're not motivated by God's kind of love it'll profit you nothing. (1 Cor. 13:3.) You must do things from a pure heart of love.

A Darkened Understanding

So when Romans 1:21 speaks of your heart becoming "darkened," it's talking about becoming insensitive to God. You are no longer responsive. You aren't hearing the voice of God. It's talking about a hardened heart.

> This I say therefore, and testify in the Lord, that ye henceforth walk not as other Gentiles walk, in the vanity of their mind, having the *understanding* darkened....
>
> EPHESIANS 4:17,18

Understanding is the same Greek word as *imagination.*[1] It's your imagination that enables you to understand. So, imagination equals understanding.

> ...being alienated from the life of God through the ignorance that is in them, because of *the blindness of their heart.*
>
> EPHESIANS 4:18

"Their foolish heart was darkened" in Romans 1:21 is saying the same thing as having your heart blinded here. It's talking about your heart not being able to see, perceive, listen, and hear from God.

Original Intent

God didn't originally create us to live the way the vast majority of us do. Most of us live from our mental, emotional, and physical parts (soul and body). We feed it all this external information. We educate it and teach it how to do things. Our natural mind is the driving force in most people. We make decisions based on all of this external, natural information we gather through our five senses. God didn't create human beings to live this way.

He did give us the capacity to process natural information. That's important when you're driving a car, for instance. If the light turns red, you need to be able to react to that and stop. But God never intended our natural man to be our driving force.

Mankind was originally created in fellowship with God. He spoke to us in our spirit because our heart—spirit—was in constant communion with Him. We were totally led by the spirit. Our heart dictated what we thought, felt, and did. When man sinned against God, that communion was broken and our spirit died. It didn't cease to exist and function. It just became separated from God. That's what the word "death" means in Scripture—separation.

There is no such thing as "ceasing to exist" in the Bible. When someone dies, their body turns to dust, but they don't cease to exist. They separate from their body. When the Word talks about us being dead in trespasses and sin (Eph. 2:1), we're still functioning—but we're separated from God.

Once that happened, we were separated from God until He provided the way back into communion. Instead of hearing the Lord and following Him, people just started ruling their own lives based on this external information. However, as born-again believers, we have access once again to letting our heart dictate and dominate our lives instead of our carnal mind and external circumstances. (2 Cor. 5:7.) But very few Christians are doing that.

Things to Come

Jesus told us that when the Holy Spirit has come, He'll teach us all things, lead us into all truth, bring all things to our remembrance, and show us things to come. (John 14:26; 16:13.) We simply haven't drawn on our spiritual man's potential anything like we can.

As I was meditating on that scripture fifteen years ago, the Lord spoke to me and said, "You haven't really been listening to Me and letting Me show you things to come." So I started praying about it and spending time being quiet in God's presence, letting Him speak to and influence me.

At the time, I had kept my four horses on a friend's property for two or three years. Every Sunday at church, he would come up to me and say, "Oh, I'm so glad you have those horses there. I don't have to mow it anymore. I just love having your horses on my property." He'd go down and feed them and play with them. Everything was going good.

As I began to ask the Lord to show me things to come, one of the first things He told me was, "You need to find a new place to put those horses." At first I thought, *But this is free and he loves having them!* It didn't make sense to me, so I waited a week.

Finally, I started asking around and found a place where I could put the horses. I'd have to pay for it, but I found something. I made the deal on Saturday and told the man, "I'm not sure when it'll be, but I know I'm going to have to move those horses."

On Sunday, this good friend of mine who owned the property my horses were on came up to me and said, "I can't stand it anymore. Those horses have to be gone by Tuesday. I will not have them anymore!" That was the first negative word he had ever spoken to me. I had no indication it was coming, except that God had prepared me. I already had the place lined up the day before he spoke to me. This was the first of many things the Lord showed me that eventually led us to where we live today.

The Lord told me eighteen months before we actually started on television that it was coming. Then two people came and prophesied it over me. This confirmed it. These are just small examples, but that's where we have to start. If you can't hear the Lord speak to you in small matters, you won't hear Him in the bigger things. Most of us wait until something external tells us, but God wants to speak to us in our heart.

Spiritually Minded

Did you know that you have two minds?

> That ye put off concerning the former conversation the old man, which is corrupt according to the deceitful lusts; and be renewed in the spirit of your mind.
>
> EPHESIANS 4:22,23

You have a natural mind and a spirit mind. It's the mind of Christ in your born-again spirit. (1 Cor. 2:16.) Again, understanding my teaching *Spirit, Soul, & Body* will really help you with this.

God will speak things to you and you can make decisions based on your spiritual mind instead of your physical mind. To most people, this sounds like I'm from another planet. They've never thought before about the fact that they have two minds. But the reason the Bible tells you not to be double-minded is because you have two minds. (James 4:8.)

You don't want to just be going back and forth between the two. You need to be spiritually minded—where your spirit mind is the master control and it just uses your natural mind as a processor. You can take natural information in, but let your spiritual mind—your heart—make the decisions. Your heart has the ability to see, hear, think, and make decisions. You should be living from your heart—not your head.

This is so hard for people to get ahold of—especially in our society where education is so exalted and esteemed. The people in charge of the news media are influencing you to be carnal. *Carnal* simply refers to the five senses. It's what you can see, taste, hear, smell, and feel. "That's what truly matters," so we are told. When you say "chili con carne," you're saying chili with meat. That's because the word "carne" is Spanish for "meat." It's where we get our English word *carnal* from. So you could say that when you're carnal, you're a meathead! You're living out of your old physical brain.

I know this sounds pretty radical to most believers, but God intended for you to live from your heart.

CHAPTER 16

Sensitive to God

"How do I live from my heart?" I'm glad you asked.

> This I say therefore, and testify in the Lord, that ye henceforth walk not as other Gentiles walk, in the vanity of their mind.
>
> EPHESIANS 4:17

"Gentile" here is talking about someone who was a non-Jew. It was someone outside of God's covenant—like a person who hasn't committed their life to the Lord Jesus Christ yet today. So this verse is saying, "Don't be like a lost person who just lives from their brain and not their heart." It's out of your heart the issues of life flow. (Prov. 4:23.) You need to learn to listen to your heart. You should be directed by your heart—not your brain.

Most Christians are living like people who don't know God and wonder why they're getting the same results. If you think like a lost person, you'll get lost person results. (Prov.

23:7.) If you start thinking like a new creation in Christ, you'll get spiritual results. (Rom. 8:6; 12:1-2.)

If you do walk in the vanity of your mind, it darkens your understanding/imagination. (Eph. 4:18.) Again, all of these things are interrelated. If you are living from your natural mind—what you can see, taste, hear, smell, and feel; and how you process that information in your little peanut brain in your head—you're going to severely limit what God can do.

When your heart becomes hardened—cold, insensitive, unfeeling, and unyielding to God—it still functions, but it automatically becomes sensitive toward physical, flesh-oriented types of things. This is where most of us live. Our hearts are conditioned to be sensitive to, dominated by, and controlled by our physical senses.

What's Your Focus?

Worry, fear, unbelief, and anger all come out of the heart.

For out of the heart proceed evil thoughts, murders, adulteries, fornications, thefts, false witness, blasphemies.

MATTHEW 15:19

For from within, out of the heart of men, proceed evil thoughts, adulteries, fornications, murders, thefts, covetousness, wickedness, deceit, lasciviousness, an evil eye, blasphemy, pride, foolishness.

MARK 7:21,22

These are products of your heart. And the reason it's responding this way is because you're letting it be dominated by all these external, physical things. Your understanding is darkened, so you become insensitive to God. He's transmitting and speaking to you, but you don't hear because your heart is insensitive.

Your heart becomes sensitive to whatever you focus your attention on, and your heart becomes hardened to whatever you neglect. If you would glorify, magnify, and value God, then you would put a greater priority upon the Lord and His Word. He would occupy more of your focus and attention than other things. If you start being thankful, you'll humble yourself and direct your attention away from negative things and put it on positive things. This places all of your attention on God—and you become sensitive to whatever you focus your attention upon. If you glorify and thank God, your imagination will start seeing godly things instead of the negative. The end result is your heart becomes sensitive to God. This isn't hard—it's easy!

But if you're neglecting the things of God and listening to the doubt, unbelief, fear, anger, criticism, and negativity of the world, there is no way your heart will be sensitive to

Him. You can still retain knowledge, but it isn't dominating you anymore. You're insensitive because of the condition of your heart.

Refuse to Empower

How do you keep your heart sensitive to the Lord? Glorify God. Put more value on Him than anything else. This also means you have to put more attention on Him than anything else, and become thankful. Constantly rehearse your victories, remember things, and force your imagination in a positive direction. Recognize that your imagination is where things are conceived. If you don't want something birthed in you, don't think it.

Your imagination is where thoughts take on power. You can't keep thoughts from coming to you, but you can refuse to empower them. Someone spit in my face once while I was witnessing to them. It was a big wad of stuff. Do you know what? I had a thought—but it was a fleeting thought. I just kept witnessing to them and never missed a beat with what I was saying. I refused to empower it.

Thoughts will come at times, but when you let them enter into your imagination and start seeing them is when they become empowered. Stop those thoughts before they ever become imagination. You can't allow your imagination to follow a train of thought that is contrary to God's Word. This is an important truth.

If you'll do these things, you'll find it will sensitize your heart toward the Lord.

Let Peace Rule

Once you really experience God's kind of love, what the world calls "love" is just cheap in comparison. I walk in love. I don't get angry with people. If I find myself operating in unforgiveness or criticizing someone, I immediately go to the Lord about it and say, "Father, something is wrong because this isn't the way Your kind of love is." At the first sign of something like this, I'll separate myself and spend time in the Word seeking God. I'll get myself back into that position of feeling God's kind of love—even for people who hate me.

> Let the peace of God rule in your hearts.
>
> COLOSSIANS 3:15

I use Colossians 3:15 constantly. I don't allow myself to become stressed out in traffic trying to get somewhere in a hurry. I'll even pull over on the side of the road if I have to because I am not going to get out of peace. I don't get anxious either. I see other people running to catch their plane in airports. I'll just walk—and if I miss it, I miss it. It doesn't matter to me. But I refuse to get out of peace over things. I value peace highly. If anything starts making me anxious and upset, I change whatever is going on in my life in a hurry.

"Well Andrew, you wouldn't last ten minutes in the life I live." That's your fault. I wouldn't work a job that took my peace away.

There are two ways to approach this. If you don't know how to walk in peace, you'll be stressed out no matter what the situation is. But if you truly are in a bad situation that's stealing your peace, you need to change that situation. That's not healthy for you—physically or spiritually.

I just don't live in anything that takes my peace away. I don't do things like that. This is why I don't go to certain places to minister. I know it's not a godly situation. I make a lot of decisions based on peace.

"I'm Not Coming"

In 1980, I was planning on going to Central America. I had been there before and saw awesome results. I'd already bought the tickets and everything was set up, but I lost my peace about it. At the time, I was moving my mother from Texas to Colorado. I prayed about this Central American trip while driving the U-haul truck for seventeen hours. The more I prayed in tongues, the more I didn't like it and didn't want to go. I just didn't have any peace about it.

First of all, I checked to see if I was truly meditating on the Lord. Well, after seventeen hours of praying in tongues, I knew I was meditating on the Lord. But I still didn't have any peace. The more I prayed about it, the less peace I had. Finally, I just called these people up and said, "I don't know what the situation is, but I'm not coming."

I cancelled that trip because I didn't have any peace about it. Later on, I found out that the plane I was scheduled to be on had taken off from Mexico City, crashed, and killed all 169 people on impact. I was preserved because I listened to my heart and kept my peace.

God speaks to you through your heart. You need to let your heart begin to dominate you. However, if you aren't glorifying God, being thankful, and your imagination has become vain, then your foolish heart will be darkened. (Rom. 1:21.) In other words, it's blind. You're alienated from the life of God within you because of the hardness and dullness of your heart. (Eph. 4:18.) This is where most Christians are because they haven't been seeking God, putting value on Him, praising His name, and using their imaginations properly. They're so dull and insensitive to God that they can't hear Him speaking to them constantly.

"Pull Over and Park"

John G. Lake was driving up a mountain road. As he went around this sharp left-hand curve with a thousand foot drop-off, the Lord said, "Pull into the left lane and park." That doesn't make sense. If you pulled into the left lane on a mountain road during a sharp left-hand curve, anybody coming down the other way would run right into you. I hear the voice of God, but I'm not quite that sensitive yet. I probably would have wanted three visions and a confirmation, and been two miles up the road before I responded. But Lake just instantly pulled over and parked.

Within seconds, a log truck came barreling out of control down the mountain. It couldn't handle the curve and was over in the outside lane. If Lake hadn't been parked where he was on the inside, he would have collided with that log truck and both of them would have gone off the mountain and been destroyed.

God is no respecter of persons. He speaks to everyone every time anything is about to go wrong in our life. He speaks, but if our heart is darkened, we're alienated from that life—that voice of God—because of the hardness of our heart.

Many people wondered why God "allowed" Keith Green, a Christian singer and song writer, to die. He took off in a small airplane and hit some high wires. When the plane crashed, the pilot, Keith, and two of his children were killed. Keith's wife had a dream that the plane was going to crash. She begged Keith not to fly. The pilot even told him the plane was overweight and they shouldn't fly, but Keith prevailed.

God speaks to us all the time. I've heard testimonies of people whom God told not to get on the freeway and something major happened. It's not God who is unfaithful, it's us who don't hear His voice because we aren't letting our heart dominate and lead us. Instead, we're just going along in the ignorance and blindness of our mind.

Perfect Wisdom

Your mind doesn't have near the capacity for understanding and processing things that your heart does. Your heart is where the real wisdom lies. As a born-again believer, you "have the mind of Christ" (1 Cor. 2:16) and the Bible says to:

> Put on the new *man* [your spirit man], which is renewed in knowledge after the image of him that created him.
>
> COLOSSIANS 3:10

Even in the natural realm, experts say that we only use 10 percent of our brain. I believe that if you were using 100 percent of your brain, it still wouldn't be able to compete with just 10 percent of your spiritual mind. Your spiritual mind has the mind of Christ in it!

> Ye have an unction from the Holy One, and ye know all things.
>
> 1 JOHN 2:20

That's not talking about your natural mind. Your last test score proves that. It's your spirit—not your brain—that knows all things. In your born-again spirit, you have the perfect wisdom and mind of Christ. You know all things in your spirit. But if you allow your heart to become darkened, what good is all of this wisdom and God speaking to you if you can't perceive it? God speaks to you through your heart.

Head or Heart?

We have this tremendous presence of God in our heart, but most of us aren't listening. He speaks to us in a still, small voice, but we're listening to all these external things instead and our little natural mind is trying to figure out how to make our life work. If you don't get to the place where you honestly trust your heart more than your head, you're never going to become a successful Christian.

My son, attend to my words; incline thine ear unto my sayings. Let them not depart from thine eyes; keep them in the midst of thine heart.

PROVERBS 4:20,21

Where do you keep God's Word? In the midst of your heart!

Thy word have I hid in mine heart, that I might not sin against thee.

PSALM 119:11

For they *are* life unto those that find them, and health to all their flesh. Keep thy heart with all diligence; for out of it *are* the issues of life.

PROVERBS 4:22,23

Life comes from your heart—not your mind or external things. You need to keep your heart with all diligence. This means putting a priority on your heart and making sure it's the most important thing.

We educate our brain. We even have laws that if you don't go to school, you're truant and they'll prosecute you. So you get up, drag yourself out of bed, and make yourself go to school. You make yourself do things. But when it comes to your spiritual life, you'd like to study the Word more, fellowship with God more, and pray in the Spirit more, but that's only if everything else isn't too pressing and you have enough time. You attend church if you feel like it. Most of us haven't put the priority on seeking the wisdom that's already in our spirit and drawing on that life. We haven't put God first place in our heart—and we wonder why we aren't receiving better results. Our lifestyle simply isn't conducive to really walking with God.

Sit and Soak

Sadhu Sundar Singh was a Hindu holy man in India. He had a vision and was converted to the Lord. He went to Bombay once (called Mumbai today) and saw something like fifteen or twenty people raised from the dead in one day. This guy saw hundreds of people raised from the dead! He had half a million people at his meetings in India, and finally had to quit praying for the sick because there were so many people to pray for that he never had an opportunity to preach the gospel. So he quit praying for the sick because he felt that preaching the gospel was more important. Great things happened. When I went to India, everyone knew about Sadhu Sundar Singh. He's a legend over there. He died in about 1929.

Around 1920, he came over to the United States. It took a month or two for him to get here by boat. He got off the ship in New York City, spent thirty minutes walking around, got back on the boat, cancelled all of his appointments, and said, "These people will never listen to the gospel. They're too busy!" That was 1920! Can you imagine what he would think of our lifestyle today?

> Be still, and know that I *am* God.
>
> PSALM 46:10

It takes time to meditate and give all diligence to your heart. You can't say, "I give quality time. It's only five minutes a day, but it's quality." You have to have some quantity time too. You need to sit and soak in the presence of God.

That's the reason for extended meetings. If we had a meeting sometime that just went for a whole month, by the end of that time you'd see things happen that you would never see in a three or four day meeting. Why? Because people would have just sat and soaked. If you could get people to commit that much time to come, sit under the Word, and soak in God's awesome presence, it would transform the way they received.

You have to start spending time in God's presence listening to your heart and paying attention to the Lord speaking to you. God doesn't work like a microwave. You can't microwave your miracle. You need to spend time sitting in the presence of the Lord. There's just no shortcut to it.

CHAPTER 17

Meditate on the Word

"How do I get understanding? How do I train my heart so it can listen and see?" God's Word tells us how:

I have more understanding than all my teachers: for thy testimonies *are* my meditation.

PSALM 119:99

What is meditation? It's reading the Word, then closing your physical eyes and thinking about what you've read until you can see it with the spiritual eyes of your heart—your imagination.

Inside First, Then Outside

John 14:12 is a powerful verse, but you need to see it in your heart before you can experience it for yourself.

Verily, verily, I say unto you, He that believeth on me, the works that I do shall he do also; and greater *works* than these shall he do; because I go unto my Father.

Don't just read it and move on—stop and think about it. Sit down, close your Bible, and pray, "Lord, this says that as a believer in You, I will do the same works You did—and even greater." Ponder yourself doing the works that Jesus did. With your mind, start seeing yourself healing the sick, cleansing the lepers, and expelling demons. See yourself laying hands on someone who's dead and see them come back to life. See the blind receiving sight and the deaf hearing. Then say, "That's what Jesus told me to do. Since I'm a believer, I'm going to see these things come to pass."

If you would meditate on that, you'd have more understanding than all of your teachers. Your spirit would begin to open up and you'd start seeing things with your heart. You'd hear God speaking to you in your heart and leading you to do certain things. This is how it works.

Until you see it on the inside, you can't see it on the outside.

"What Am I Preaching?"

I used John 14:12 to preach a message in a Wednesday night service once in Corpus Christi, Texas. I left the next day, but the pastor had listened and meditated on that verse the rest of the week. On Sunday morning, he stood up and preached on John 14:12 again, saying, "We're going to see the dead raised. I've been meditating on this and I've conceived something on the inside. I just know it's going to happen!"

While he was preaching this, a man stood up on the side, walked forward, grabbed his heart, and fell over dead. They had a nurse in the audience. She came up, checked his vitals, and said, "He's dead. There's no pulse." They tried CPR. They called the fire station, which—by the way—was just across the street. Normally, the emergency personnel would have been there almost instantaneously. But this time it took them twenty-five minutes.

Since they had already tried CPR, the guy was gone, and the service was ruined, the pastor didn't know what to do. With this dead man laying at the front of the church, he finally said, "Let's pray." As they started to pray, he exclaimed, "What am I preaching? We're going to see the dead raised. This guy is dead." So he walked over and spoke to him, and this guy rose up from the dead—right as the paramedics walked in!

After taking him to the hospital and examining him, they declared him totally healthy and let him go. This guy had to catch a taxi back to the church. He made the pastor pay the fare, saying, "I didn't want to go to the hospital in the first place. You made me go!" So they saw this man raised from the dead.

How did that happen? First of all, they started meditating on that Word.

Exercise Your Mind

I'm not trying to scold anyone. I just want to make it clear that God isn't our problem. We're our problem. Very few believers meditate on the Word day and night like it says to in Joshua 1:8. "Come on Andrew, not everyone is a preacher like you. Somebody has to work. I can't meditate on the Word day and night." Yes, you can.

The same part of you that worries also meditates. Worry is nothing but meditation on something bad. You can meditate on the things of God and still do your job. In fact, you'll do it even better. You can keep your mind stayed on God. You can bring every thought into captivity and under obedience to Christ. You don't have to be a minister to meditate on the Word day and night.

Most preachers are on call twenty-four hours a day and they have so many things coming at them. It's hard to spend time meditating on the Word when you're a minister. There are so many other things that need to be done. So don't give me this "It doesn't work for everyone else" junk. The Bible says that you can bring every thought into captivity and under obedience. (2 Cor. 10:5.) God wouldn't have commanded you to meditate on the Word day and night if you couldn't do it. You can do it.

Our minds are like a muscle that hasn't been exercised. In some people, they're nearly atrophied. We sit down in front of a television and turn it on and let it do the thinking for us so we won't have to put forth any effort. Reading the newspaper is too much effort for some folks. We just want to sit down and have someone give it to us intravenously. It takes time and effort to exercise your mind. But you can get to a place where it'll respond to you and do what you want it to. You can exercise your mind.

Read With Your Heart

Through thy precepts I get understanding: therefore I hate every false way.

PSALM 119:104

God's Word gives you understanding. It opens up your heart.

The entrance of thy words giveth light; it giveth understanding unto the simple.

PSALM 119:130

God's Word touches your heart. Some people struggle with the Word because they're trying to understand it with their brain. But God's Word is written to your heart. If you'll read it with your heart, you'll have understanding. If you just try to pick it apart with your brain, you'll mess up and miss things. God's Word is written on your heart. If you'll listen, the entrance of His Word will give you light. It gives understanding to the simple.

The purpose of the book of Proverbs is:

> To know wisdom and instruction; to perceive the words of understanding; to receive the instruction of wisdom, justice, and judgment, and equity; to give subtlety to the simple, to the young man knowledge and discretion. A wise *man* will hear, and will increase learning; and a man of understanding shall attain unto wise counsels: to understand a proverb, and the interpretation; the words of the wise, and their dark sayings.
>
> PROVERBS 1:2-6

The book of Proverbs was written to give you God's wisdom and understanding. If you don't have it, take Proverbs and read it. Put your finger on a particular verse or passage and say, "Lord, You said You'd give me wisdom and understanding. I open my heart to Your Word." Then meditate on it, and it'll give you more understanding than all of your teachers.

The Principal Thing

> My son, if thou wilt receive my words, and hide my commandments with thee; so that thou incline thine ear unto

wisdom, *and* apply thine heart to understanding; yea, if thou criest after knowledge, *and* liftest up thy voice for understanding; if thou seekest her as silver, and searchest for her as *for*hid treasures.

PROVERBS 2:1-4

Sometimes we spiritualize things and miss this, but this means that you ought to desire God's Word more than seeing your business prosper. When you get to the point where you want wisdom more than you want money, you'll get it.

If thou seekest her as silver, and searchest for her as *for* hid treasures; then shalt thou understand the fear of the LORD, and find the knowledge of God. For the LORD giveth wisdom: out of his mouth *cometh*knowledge and understanding.

PROVERBS 2:4-6

Out of His mouth is the Word of God.

Discretion shall preserve thee, understanding shall keep thee.

PROVERBS 2:11

Wisdom *is* the principal thing; *therefore* get wisdom: and with all thy getting get understanding.

PROVERBS 4:7

This isn't just talking about carnal knowledge, but an attitude of the heart. Understanding is a function of the heart.

Adulterers and Animals

But whoso committeth adultery with a woman lacketh understanding: he *that* doeth it destroyeth his own soul.

PROVERBS 6:32

Be ye not as the horse, *or* as the mule, *which* have no understanding: whose mouth must be held in with bit and bridle, lest they come near unto thee.

PSALM 32:9

Don't act like an animal that has no understanding. They have to have something in their mouth causing them pain in order to restrain them. All they respond to is something physical. You need to be able to listen to your heart, have understanding, and not be punished physically.

I'm amazed how many people don't follow this. Don't wait to listen to your spirit until things are going wrong, your marriage falls apart, and everything in the natural is crashing and burning. If you make that a habit, you'll be someone who is constantly going from pit to pit instead of glory to glory. You need to listen to your heart.

If you're out committing adultery, you lack understanding. You aren't listening to your heart. You're just like a horse—letting your hormones drive you.

Horses aren't stupid, but they can't reason and understand—especially when a stallion's hormones start flowing. There is simply no reason to it whatsoever. I know. I've had one before. Once that stallion's hormones started raging, he always made a beeline straight to the nearest mare no matter who or what stood in his way. He was totally insensitive to anything other than his hormones and that mare.

Access to Change

A person who commits adultery is just like that. They're brain dead. They aren't listening to God or their heart. They aren't sensitive to that inner witness. They've fallen out of communion with God.

If you were to get to the place where your heart ruled, it would be impossible for you to commit adultery. You have to literally shut off your heart before you can do something like that. You can't be in communion with God and act that way. This isn't just true of adultery; it's true of a thousand things. If you were in communion with God, you couldn't be so selfish, angry, mean, or depressed. You couldn't be a lot of things that you are if you'd just be in communion with God.

The four keys I've shared in this book are progressive steps that lead to an established heart. First, we value God and what He has said and done in our life. Second, we are thankful, which involves remembering. Third, we use our imagination in a positive way, and if we've done all of those things, then our heart just naturally becomes sensitive to God. But failure to do the first three things will make it impossible for your heart to be sensitive toward the Lord.

So often, we're trying to change our behavior without first changing our heart. Our heart is filled with all this junk. We're thinking on the wrong things. We're cold and insensitive toward God. This is how our heart is, but we want different results. That's the wrong way to fix this problem.

What I'm sharing may not be the easiest, but it's how God designed us. Most people would like to come forward, have somebody lay hands on them, and cast out their desire to commit adultery, their depression, or whatever. We want instantaneous results and we don't want to have to do something that takes effort. Although it takes more time and effort to change your heart and get it established, once it's changed it also takes time to get out of it. Once you start acting right from the heart, you won't find yourself falling into sin. Once your heart is established, it'll direct you.

You can't change your heart for the good without glorifying God, being thankful, and using your imagination in a positive way. This is how you access your heart. This is how you begin to change.

Conclusion

This process revealed in Romans 1:21 doesn't work backwards. You must start from the beginning.

Make a conscious decision to glorify God. Place more value on the Lord, what He's said, and what He's done in your life than anything or anyone else. Don't let them even compete.

You can't want the acclaim of people. You can't be codependent on your spouse, children, or job. You have to get to the place where your love for and commitment to God stands alone. Even if everything else in your life fell apart, you'd still esteem, honor, and put more importance on Him. You can stand on God's Word alone.

Magnify the Lord and make Him bigger. Praise Him, thank Him, and rehearse your victories. Make a conscious effort to minimize the negative, despise the shame, set joy before you, and fix your eyes on the good things God has done. If you'll do this, your imagination will start seeing positive things and your heart will become sensitized to God.

These are the steps you must take. There is no other way to get there. It really is that simple.

This is how God made your heart. It's how He designed you to function. You may not like it. You might want a different way of doing it. But according to His Word, this is how the Lord made you. It's how He set it up.

If you give priority to these things, it'll save your life. If you listen to and follow your heart, you'll walk in supernatural wisdom and peace. God will speak to you about these things, but you must practice what you've learned.

Listen to Your Heart

We have our annual Andrew Wommack Ministries board meeting every January. While I was packing for it last year, I asked the Lord if I had forgotten anything. You might think, "Come on Andrew, that's why God gave you a brain." Well, I don't believe it bothers the Lord. I just ask Him to remind me of things.

Personally, I don't use an alarm clock. I just ask the Lord to wake me up. I'm not saying it's wrong for you to use one. I just choose not to because it keeps me listening to God. I make myself live in such a way that I have to be dependent on God. I've gone to bed with only two hours to sleep and had to get up in order to catch an international flight I couldn't miss. I just asked Him to wake me up on time, and He did. You don't have to do this. There are different ways to accomplish the same thing. This is just how I've chosen to do it. I listen to my heart and the Lord always wakes me up. I've never missed a flight!

So in getting ready for that board meeting, I asked the Lord if there was something else I needed to take. My eyes fell upon a Denver Broncos Super Bowl Champion hat that someone had given to me. I thought to myself, *I bet one of my board members would like that hat.* Believing that was the Lord, I packed it without saying anything to anyone.

After the board meeting, we were all getting ready to leave. I was out at my car saying goodbye, when one of my board members who lives in Oregon asked, "Do you know where I can get one of those Broncos hats? I've been wanting one and have tried two or three different places, but I just can't find one."

I replied, "Well, I just happen to have one right here" and gave it him. This just encouraged me that the Holy Spirit will show you things if you'll listen in your heart.

I actually believe that's a part of me operating in the gifts of the Spirit. If I can't hear things like that, how am I going to hear God say, "There's someone here who's been wanting to commit suicide" and things like that? Don't just listen to God during your devotions and operate in the flesh the rest of the day. It's not right to compartmentalize your life that way.

What Are You Going to Do?

God will help you do whatever it is you do. He'll make you a better accountant. He'll show you where the errors are and make things work. God will make you a better truck driver. He'll show you when things are coming up. There isn't anything you can do that you can't do better being sensitive and listening to God.

We've really messed it up by operating entire parts of our life carnally. God didn't make us to function that way.

As you start listening to your heart, you'll be amazed by what God will do through you. This isn't the easiest way, but it's the best. You need to get your heart established. It really is that simple.

If you receive these four keys to staying full of God and start implementing them in your daily life, you'll experience a radical transformation. This could change your life forever, but it all depends on what you do with it. What value will you place on what you've learned? Only you can decide.

Welcome to Your New Life!

Choosing to receive Jesus Christ as your Lord and Savior is the most important decision you'll ever make.

God's Word promises, "That if thou shalt confess with thy mouth the Lord Jesus, and shalt believe in thine heart that God hath raised him from the dead, thou shalt be saved. For with the heart man believeth unto righteousness; and with the mouth confession is made unto salvation" (Rom. 10:9-10).

> For whosoever shall call upon the name of the Lord shall be saved.
>
> ROMANS 10:13

By His grace, God has already done everything to provide salvation. Your part is simply to believe and receive.

Pray out loud, *"Jesus, I confess that You are my Lord and Savior. I believe in my heart that God raised You from the dead. By faith in Your Word, I receive salvation now. Thank You for saving me!"*

The very moment you commit your life to Jesus Christ, the truth of His Word instantly comes to pass in your spirit. Now that you're born again, there's a brand-new you!

As His child, your loving heavenly Father wants to give you the supernatural power you need to live this new life.

> For every one that asketh receiveth; and he that seeketh findeth; and to him that knocketh it shall be opened...how much more shall *your* heavenly Father give the Holy Spirit to them that ask him?
>
> LUKE 11:10,13

All you have to do is ask, believe, and receive.

Pray, *"Father, I recognize my need for Your power to live this new life. Please fill me with Your Holy Spirit. By faith, I receive it right now. Thank You for baptizing me. Holy Spirit, You are welcome in my life."*

Congratulations—now you're filled with God's supernatural power!

Some syllables from a language you don't recognize will rise up from your heart to your mouth. As you speak them out loud by faith, you're releasing God's power from within and building yourself up in the spirit. (1 Cor. 14:4,14.) You can do this whenever and wherever you like.

It doesn't really matter whether you felt anything or not when you prayed to receive the Lord and His Spirit. If you believed in your heart that you received, then God's Word promises you did. "Therefore I say unto you, What things soever ye desire, when ye pray, believe that ye receive *them*, and ye shall have *them*" (Mark 11:24). God always honors His Word—believe it!

Please contact me if you prayed either one or both of these prayers. I'd like to rejoice with you and send you a free gift that will help you understand and grow in your new relationship with the Lord. It's just my way of saying, *"Welcome to your new life!"*

ENDNOTES

Chapter 1

[1] Thayer and Smith, *The KJV New Testament Greek Lexicon,* "Greek Lexicon entry for Euaggelion," available from http://www.biblestudytools.net/Lexicons/Greek/grk.cgi?number =2098&version=kjv, s.v. "gospel," Romans 1:16.

[2] Ibid.

Chapter 2

[1] James Strong, *Strong's Exhaustive Concordance of the Bible,* "New Strong's Concise Dictionary of the Words in the Greek Testament," #1392, p. 24, s.v. "glorified," Romans 1:21.

[2] Based on information from *Noah Webster's Dictionary of American English,* available from http://www.e-sword.net/dictionaries.html, s.v. "esteem."

[3] James Strong, #2706, p. 48, s.v. "despised," Hebrews 12:2.

Chapter 4

[1] Thayer and Smith, *The KJV New Testament Greek Lexicon,* "Greek Lexicon entry for Doxazo," available from http://www.bible studytools.net/Lexicons/Greek/grk.cgi?number=1392&version= kjv, s.v. "glorify," and "magnify," Romans 1:21; 11:13.

Chapter 6

[1] Thayer and Smith, *The KJV New Testament Greek Lexicon,* "Greek Lexicon entry for Apoblepo," available from http://www.biblestudytools.net/Lexicons/Greek/grk.cgi?number =578&version=kjv, s.v. "respect," Hebrews 11:26.

2 Ibid., "Greek Lexicon entry for Hegeomai," available from http://www.biblestudytools.net/Lexicons/Greek/grk.cgi?number=2233&version=kjv, s.v. "count," Philippians 3:7-8.

3 Ibid., s.v. "esteeming," Hebrews 11:26.

Chapter 8

1 Brown, Driver, Briggs and Gesenius, *The KJV Old Testament Hebrew Lexicon*, "Hebrew Lexicon entry for Towtsa'ah," available from http://www.biblestudytools.net/Lexicons/Hebrew/heb.cgi?number=8444&version=kjv, s.v. "issues," Psalm 68:20.

Chapter 9

1 There is much information available that substantiates this statement, including an article by Michael Yapko, *Psychology Today,* "Advice: The Brain and Depression," available from http://www.psychologytoday.com/articles/pto-20040521-000010.html.

Chapter 10

1 Thayer and Smith, *The KJV New Testament Greek Lexicon,* "Greek Lexicon entry for Euodia," available from http://www.biblestudytools.net/Lexicons/Greek/grk.cgi?number=2175&version=kjv, s.v. "savour," 2 Corinthians 2:15.

2 Brown, Driver, Briggs and Gesenius, *The KJV Old Testament Hebrew Lexicon,* "Hebrew Lexicon entry for Yetser," available from http://www.biblestudytools.net/Lexicons/Hebrew/heb.cgi?number=3336&version=kjv, s.v. "imaginations," 1 Chronicles 28:9.

3 Based on information from *Noah Webster's Dictionary of American English,* available from http://www.e-sword.net/dictionaries.html, s.v. "conception," 1 Chronicles 28:9.

Chapter 11

[1] Brown, Driver, Briggs and Gesenius, *The KJV Old Testament Hebrew Lexicon,* "Hebrew Lexicon entry for Yetser," available from http://www.biblestudytools.net/Lexicons/Hebrew/heb.cgi?number=3336&version=kjv, s.v. "mind," Isaiah 26:3.

Chapter 13

[1] Thayer and Smith, *The KJV New Testament Greek Lexicon,* "Greek Lexicon entry for Blepo," available from http://www.study-light.org/lex/grk/view.cgi?number=991.

[2] Based on information from the *Online Etymology Dictionary,* available from http://www.etymonline.com/index.php?term=ana-.

[3] Thayer and Smith, *The KJV New Testament Greek Lexicon,* "Greek Lexicon entry for Anablepo," available from http://www.biblestudytools.net/Lexicons/Greek/grk.cgi?number=308&version=kjv.

[4] Ibid.

[5] Ibid.

Chapter 15

[1] Thayer and Smith, *The KJV New Testament Greek Lexicon,* "Greek Lexicon entry for Dianoia," available from http://www.biblestudytools.net/Lexicons/Greek/grk.cgi?number=1271&version=kjv, s.v. "understanding" and "imagination," Ephesians 4:18.

We Would Like to Hear From You

If you have prayed the salvation prayer for the first time, or if you have a testimony to share after reading this book, please send us an email at **www.harrisonhouse.com**.

Or you may write to us at:

Harrison House Publishers
P.O. Box 35035
Tulsa, Oklahoma 745153

About the Author

For over three decades Andrew Wommack has traveled America and the world teaching the truth of the Gospel. His profound revelation of the Word of God is taught with clarity and simplicity, emphasizing God's unconditional love and the balance between grace and faith. He reaches millions of people through the daily *Gospel Truth* radio and television programs, broadcast both domestically and internationally. He founded Charis Bible College in 1994 and has since established CBC extension schools in other major cities of America and around the world. Andrew has produced a library of teaching materials, available in print, audio, and visual formats. And, as it has been from the beginning, his ministry continues to distribute free audiotapes and CDs to those who cannot afford them.

To contact Andrew Wommack please write, email, or call:

Andrew Wommack Ministries, Inc.
P.O. Box 3333 • Colorado Springs, CO 80934-3333
E-mail: awommack@aol.com
Helpline Phone (orders and prayer): (719) 635-1111
Hours: 4:00 AM to 9:30 PM MST

Andrew Wommack Ministries of Europe
P.O. Box 4392 • WS1 9AR Walsall • ENGLAND
E-mail: enquiries@awme.net
UK Helpline Phone (orders and prayer):
011-44-192-247-3300
Hours: 5:30 AM to 4:00 PM GMT

Or visit him on the web at:
www.awmi.net

You've Already Got It!

Have you ever thought, *I'm doing everything I know to do, what's wrong with me? What's it going to take to get God to move on my behalf?* If you have, you're not alone. It's a question most Christians ask and yet remain frustrated with the answers they receive.

The answers usually go something like this: If you will pray a little longer and with more sincerity, spend more time fasting, read a few more chapters in the Bible every day, and quit wasting time in front of the television, then God will answer your prayers. He's just waiting for you to shape up.

In other words, your performance is the problem. The fact is, that couldn't be further from the truth. *You've Already Got It!* is a book filled with the good news that God's response isn't based on the things you must do; it's based on what Jesus did. As you read, you'll gain the knowledge to trust God. It's only the truth you know that will set you free!

Item Code: 1033-C 6-CD album

ISBN: 1-57794-833-5
Paperback

You've Already Got It
Unabridged Audio Book
6 CDs
ISBN 978-1-57794-995-4

Grace, The Power of the Gospel

Recent surveys indicate that the vast majority of Christians, those claiming to be born-again, believe that their salvation is at least in part dependent upon their behavior and actions. Yes, they believe Jesus died for their sin, but once they accept Him as their Savior they believe they must still meet a certain standard to be "good" enough.

If that is true, then what is that standard and how do you know when you have met it? The Church has tried to answer these questions for centuries and it always results in religious and legalistic bondage.

So what is the answer? It begins by asking the right question. It is not, "What must we do?" but rather, "What did Jesus do?" By understanding the Apostle Paul's revelation of what Jesus did from the book of Romans, you will never again wonder if you're meeting the standard.

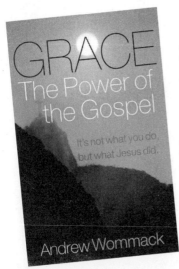

Item Code: 1014-C
4-CD album

ISBN: 978-1-57794-921-3
Paperback

A Better Way to Pray

After nearly four decades of ministry, Andrew has asked God many questions about prayer and discovered some important truths through the Scriptures. His prayer life is much different than it was thirty years ago and the results have dramatically improved!

The principles found in this book may not be the only way to pray, but if you are not getting the results you desire, consider changing directions; maybe there is *A Better Way to Pray*.

Item Code: 1042-C 5-CD album

ISBN: 1-57794-834-6
Paperback

A Better Way to Pray
Unabridged Audio Book
4 CDs
ISBN 978-157794-994-7

OTHER TEACHINGS BY ANDREW WOMMACK

Spirit, Soul & Body

Understanding the relationship of your spirit, soul, and body is foundational to your Christian life. You will never truly know how much God loves you or believe what His Word says about you until you do. In this series, learn how they're related and how that knowledge will release the life of your spirit into your body and soul. It may even explain why many things are not working the way you had hoped.

Item Code: 318-Paperback

Item Code: 1027-C 4-CD album

The True Nature of God

Are you confused about the nature of God? Is He the God of judgment found in the Old Testament, or the God of mercy and grace found in the New Testament? Andrew's revelation on this subject will set you free and give you a confidence in your relationship with God like never before. This is truly nearly-too-good-to-be-true news.

Item Code: 308-Paperback

Item Code: 1002-C 5-CD album

Living in the Balance of Grace and Faith

This book explains one of the biggest controversies in the church today. Is it grace or faith that releases the power of God? Does God save people in His sovereignty, or does your faith move Him? You may be surprised by the answers as Andrew reveals what the Bible has to say concerning these important questions and more. This will help you receive from God in a greater way and will change the way you relate to Him.

Item Code: 301B-Paperback

The Believer's Authority

Like it or not, every one of us is in a spiritual war. You can't be discharged from service, and ignorance of the battlefield only aids the enemy. In war, God is always for us, and the devil is against us; whichever one we cooperate with will win. And there's only one way the enemy can get your cooperation—that's through deception. In this teaching, Andrew exposes this war and the enemy for what he is.

Item Code: 1045-C 6-CD album

Item Code: 1045-D 6-DVD album

(as recorded from television)

The Effects of Praise

Every Christian wants a stronger walk with the Lord. But how do you get there? Many don't know the true power of praise. It's essential. Listen as Andrew teaches biblical truths that will not only spark understanding but will help promote spiritual growth so you will experience victory.

Item Code: 309-Paperback

Item Code: 1004-C 3-CD album

God Wants You Well

Health is something everyone wants. Billions of dollars are spent each year trying to retain or restore health. So why does religion tell us that God uses sickness to teach us something? It even tries to make us believe that sickness is a blessing. That's just not true. God wants you well!

Item Code: 1036-C 4-CD album

Fast. Easy.
Convenient.

For the latest Harrison House product information and author news, look no further than your computer. All the details on our powerful, life-changing products are just a click away. New releases, E-mail subscriptions, Podcasts, testimonies, monthly specials—find it all in one place. Visit harrisonhouse.com today!

harrisonhouse

The Harrison House Vision

Proclaiming the truth and the power

Of the Gospel of Jesus Christ

With excellence;

Challenging Christians to

Live victoriously,

Grow spiritually,

Know God intimately.